Claiming the Mantle

Dilemmas in American Politics

Series Editor: **L. Sandy Maisel,** Colby College

If the answers to the problems facing U.S. democracy were easy, politicians would solve them, accept credit, and move on. But certain dilemmas have confronted the American political system continuously. They defy solution; they are endemic to the system. Some can best be described as institutional dilemmas: How can the Congress be both a representative body and a national decision maker? How can the president communicate with more than 250 million citizens effectively? Why do we have a two-party system when many voters are disappointed with the choices presented to them? Others are policy dilemmas: How do we find compromises on issues that defy compromise, such as abortion policy? How do we incorporate racial and ethnic minorities or immigrant groups into American society, allowing them to reap the benefits of this land without sacrificing their identity? How do we fund health care for our poorest or oldest citizens?

Dilemmas such as these are what propel students toward an interest in the study of U.S. government. Each book in the *Dilemmas in American Politics* series addresses a "real-world" problem, raising the issues that are of most concern to students. Each is structured to cover the historical and theoretical aspects of the dilemma but also to explore the dilemma from a practical point of view and to speculate about the future. The books are designed as supplements to introductory courses in American politics or as case studies to be used in upper-level courses. The link among them is the desire to make the real issues confronting the political world come alive in students' eyes.

BOOKS IN THIS SERIES

Claiming the Mantle

How Presidential Nominations Are Won and Lost Before the Votes Are Cast

R. Lawrence Butler
Assistant Professor of Political Science
Rowan University, Glassboro, New Jersey

A Member of the Perseus Books Group

Copyright © 2004 by Westview Press, A Member of the Perseus Books Group.

Published in 2004 in the United States of America by Westview Press.

Find us on the world wide web at www.westviewpress.com.

Westview Press books are available at special discounts for bulk purchases in the United States by corporations, institutions, and other organizations. For more information, please contact the Special Markets Department at the Perseus Books Group, 11 Cambridge Center, Cambridge, MA 02142, or call (800) 255-1514 or (617) 252-5298, or e-mail special.markets@perseusbooks.com.

Library of Congress Cataloging-in-Publication Data
Butler, Roger Lawrence, 1963-
    Claiming the mantle : how presidential nominations are won and lost before the votes are cast / R. Lawrence Butler.
        p.   cm. — (Dilemmas in American politics)
    Includes bibliographical references and index.
    ISBN 0-8133-4208-2 (pbk. : alk. paper)
    1.Presidents—United States—Nomination. 2. Primaries—United States. I. Title. II. Series.
JK522.B88 2005
324.273'15—dc22

2004020097

The paper used in this publication meets the requirements of the American National Standard for Permanence of Paper for Printed Library Materials Z39.48–1984.

10   9   8   7   6   5   4   3   2   1

*For my wife Joanne—
who gave me the courage
to be who I was meant to be*

Contents

7 **Clash of the Titans**

....

8 **Looking Ahead**

....

PART I

THE RULES OF THE GAME

1

The Sound of Bubbles Bursting

O<small>N</small> J<small>ANUARY</small> 31, 2000, it seemed as if Christmas Eve had come again to Washington, D.C. Like a small child listening for the sound of Santa coming down the chimney with a bag full of toys, the chattering class in Washington was quivering with excitement. They had been waiting for this moment for a generation.

Not since the Democratic confab in 1980 had a presidential nominating convention opened in which there was the slightest doubt as to who the winner would be. Now, on the eve of the New Hampshire primary, both parties appeared headed for an extended showdown. On the Democratic side, the former New Jersey senator and basketball star Bill Bradley had been slugging it out with Vice President Al Gore for months. For the Republicans, Senator John McCain of Arizona, the war hero and media darling, had pulled even in some polls with Governor George W. Bush of Texas, the son of a former president. For candidates and pundits alike, hope seemed as fresh and expansive as the frozen surface of Lake Winnipesaukee after a snowfall.

At the stroke of midnight on January 31, Santa Claus arrived in the guise of the good citizens of Dixville Notch, New Hampshire, population thirty-three. Every four years, all of the registered voters of this tiny hamlet gather together for a timeless ritual of democracy—casting the first votes of the New Hampshire primary. Each voter marks a paper ballot and stuffs it into an old wooden ballot box. Minutes later, all the votes are counted. On this night, the tally was Bush 12, McCain 10, Bradley 4, Gore 2, and the publisher Steve Forbes 1. Washington political watchers happily braced themselves for a slugfest. The race had begun.

Elsewhere in America, spring is the season of hope and renewal. Flowers that have lain dormant for months burst out into vibrant colors. The eerie silence of winter is broken by the merry chirping of birds building nests to prepare for the arrival of new life. And all across the nation, optimistic baseball fans crave the sound of horsehide on leather that marks the opening day of the season in which, no doubt, their team will finally make it to the World Series.

Not so in the world of presidential politics. By the first day of spring, the dreams of the chattering class had been shattered as the McCain and Bradley campaigns lay in ruin, crushed beneath the wheels of the Bush and Gore juggernauts. Bush had clinched the nomination, having secured 987 of the 1,884 convention delegates. McCain had won only 239. Gore had defeated Bradley in all thirty Democratic primaries and caucuses held in states across the country.

How could this have happened? Did McCain and Bradley make some horrible mistakes that doomed their candidacies? The truth of the matter is that, despite the hopes of the pundits, they never had a chance of winning.

Fast-forward to the race for the 2004 Democratic presidential nomination, which began in earnest in December 2002, when Al Gore announced that he would not enter the contest. Without him in the field there was no obvious heir apparent around whom the party could coalesce. Consequently, nine challengers jumped into the race during the first quarter of 2003. Throughout the year they jockeyed back and forth, but none of them gained an overwhelming advantage. As the year 2004 opened, the media-anointed leader of the pack, Howard Dean, a former governor of Vermont, was struggling to stay ahead of several fast-rising candidates. On January 17, two days before the first real votes of the season were to be cast in the Iowa caucuses, Zogby International released the results of a poll of likely caucus participants showing that four candidates were at the top of the heap within five points of each other. Two days earlier the American Research Group had released a New Hampshire poll of likely voters in that state's first-in-the-nation primary (held eight days after Iowa) finding that a fifth candidate had closed to within five points of Dean. The race was starting to look like a real barn burner.

The shape of the 2004 Democratic nomination contest could not have been more different from what occurred in 2000. Then, we had two heavyweights from each party slugging it out in the primaries. On the Democratic side, the sitting Vice President was being challenged by a well-respected former senator. On the Republican side, Bush had soared ahead of the pack in 1999, only to face the hard-charging challenge of Senator McCain. By contrast, in 2003 and the first few weeks of

2004, there was a broad array of Democratic candidates with no clear favorite. Pundits began to salivate over the possibility that the five would battle each other all the way to the convention.

It was not to be. Though the field was different, the result was the same. By mid-February, few doubted that Senator John Kerry of Massachusetts would be the Democratic nominee. Once again, dreams of a convention struggle were dashed months before the primary process officially came to an end.

Why does the presidential nomination process always end up being a disappointment to analysts and voters alike? Voters, being rational creatures, do not tune in to the presidential campaign months and months in advance. But by the time they do turn their attention to the race, the nominees have already been chosen. Is it any wonder that polls often show great dissatisfaction among the voters with the candidates they are presented for president?

It wasn't supposed to be this way. The political reform movement of the late 1960s and early 1970s was designed to democratize the way presidential nominees were chosen. The goal of the reforms was to shift power from party bosses to party members. The change in the process for selecting a nominee is illustrated in two films about presidential selection—one before and one after the reforms. In the 1964 movie *The Best Man*, two candidates, played by Henry Fonda and Cliff Robertson, come to the national convention without having sewn up the nomination. In an effort to put their campaigns over the top, each courts the leaders of the various state delegations. If they can win the support of these governors, senators, and other party bosses, they know that the rest of the respective state delegations will follow suit. Why? Because the delegates have been handpicked for their loyalty to the party boss and will support whomever he chooses. In the end, both candidates knock each other out and the nomination is given to an obscure western governor little known by any of the delegates in the convention hall or by the voters back home—a so-called dark horse. This is the ultimate illustration of a system in which the proverbial cigar-chomping party bosses go into a smoke-filled room to select a candidate they can all agree on.

Fast-forward now to 1998 and the movie *Primary Colors*, which tells the story of a southern governor seeking the Democratic party nomination for president. We see Governor Stanton, played by John Travolta, use numerous communications techniques to win over the voters one state at a time. He holds town hall meetings with recently laid-off laborers. He jousts with his opponents in debates and broadcast interviews. He cuts television commercials lauding his own achievements and questioning the credentials of his opponents. By the end of the film, after beating the odds in primary after primary, Stanton is the only candidate left standing.

On paper, the people now choose the party nominees for president. And yet, the process seems to have come full circle. Voters theoretically get to pick the candidates, but in practice they rarely get the opportunity. In most cases, the contest is over before it has even begun. And even when the outcome remains in doubt at the time of the first caucuses and primaries, the contest is over in a few weeks after a burst of activity in a handful of states. How did the reform movement get so far away from the plan? The answer is that there was no single plan, nor a single entity that could craft a system to meet the original intent of the reformers.

Political systems have a certain organic quality about them. Procedures are put into place in order to create a process by which we choose our leaders and our leaders govern us. Once those procedures are established, individual politicians play the game according to the rules. However, since each politician wants to win the game, she will adopt strategies that maximize her abilities. The rules of the game, therefore, create incentives for the individual players. As some players adopt certain beneficial strategies, others adopt counterstrategies to regain the advantage. Before you know it, political practices have completely changed and the political system has evolved into something not anticipated by those who crafted the system in the first place. Call it the law of unintended consequences.

In the presidential nomination process, power resides in the hands of the candidates, national party leaders, state party leaders, constituency leaders, local activists, and of course the individual voters. Although these groups have many goals in common, each one also has its own unique interest. The candidate wants to win the nomination. National party leaders want to ensure that the nominee, whoever it is, is well positioned to win the general election. State party leaders want to maximize their state's influence in the selection process. Constituency leaders want assurance that the nominee has an acceptable position on their key issues. Local activists want to be on the winning team. With all of these competing goals, it is no wonder that the nomination system has evolved over time.

Add to that the fact that many of these players have the power to determine one or more aspects of the nomination rules. The candidates choose their own campaign strategies and get to pick which set of campaign finance rules they will follow. National party leaders set broad guidelines in an effort to steer the process toward an outcome beneficial to the party as a whole. State party leaders, often in conjunction with their state legislatures, decide when the nomination contest in their state will be held. In making these selections, one can be certain that each will choose the route that goes the farthest toward maximizing his own goals. And once such a change is made, the other players adjust their own strategies to fit the new environment. Eventually, a new equilibrium is reached, indicating that the system has changed fundamentally.

To understand this evolution of the presidential nomination system from its original conception of letting the voters decide to its current form in which the race is usually over before the first vote is cast, we must examine the incentives and the goals of the different players. That is the task of this book.

We begin in chapter 2 by looking at the formal rules for selecting convention delegates. These rules contain a great deal of flexibility, and each set of players has attempted to use its powers to push the system in a direction favorable to them. In chapter 3 we examine the formal rules for financing presidential nomination campaigns, beginning with the 1974 reforms. In recent years, as other aspects of the nomination process have changed, campaign finance regulations have so restricted the candidates' ability to meet the growing financial requirements of a presidential campaign that more and more of them have chosen to opt out of the system. Chapter 4 looks at the hurdles candidates must clear if they wish to be the nominee. Unless a candidate has positioned himself properly before the first primary or caucus by raising a great deal of money, building a strong national organization, courting constituency leaders and elected officials, and using the media to his advantage, he cannot win the nomination.

In part 2 we examine all thirteen contested presidential nomination campaigns from 1976 (the first cycle in which all of the reforms came into play) through 2004. The races are categorized into three types depending on how many candidates have emerged from the pre-primary phase of the campaign in a dominant position. Each type of race follows a specific pattern that has been replicated—and amplified—over the years. If either one or two candidates is dominating the field at the time of the first primaries and caucuses, the voters are superfluous because the victor is already guaranteed. If, however, no candidate is dominant, then the primaries and caucuses will determine the winner. Nonetheless, in recent campaign cycles, that determination has been made earlier and earlier in the process, by fewer and fewer voters, who pick from only a few candidates—the ones who have not already eliminated themselves from serious contention by their weak performances in the pre-primary phase.

Finally, in chapter 8 we step back to examine the consequences of this system for the American presidency. The true test of any political system is whether it leads to a desirable outcome. In this case, does the process by which we nominate our presidential candidates yield a president who is able to do the job well? We also examine a number of reform ideas to assess the likelihood of their adoption and the unintended consequences they might create. Many people may be disgusted with the current process, but is it truly fundamentally flawed, and is it fixable? Or is the modern presidential nomination process perhaps akin to an observation of Winston Churchill's: "Democracy is the worst form of government, except for all those others that have been tried."

2

The Formal Rules—
Winning Delegates

NINETEEN SIXTY-EIGHT WAS a violent and turbulent year in American politics. It was a year marked by assassinations, massive anti-war demonstrations, and urban riots. These protests arose not only out of the Vietnam conflict and the civil rights movement, but also from the Democratic presidential nomination process. Out of the ashes of this bonfire sprang the modern presidential nomination system.

In some ways, it seemed improbable that there would be a hotly con-tested Democratic nomination in 1968. Having won 61 percent of the vote in 1964, Lyndon Johnson was a strong incumbent who could be expected to win his party's nomination with little or no opposition. However, with the Vietnam conflict raging and becoming ever more unpopular, Senator Eugene McCarthy of Minnesota threw his hat into the ring in November 1967 as an antiwar candidate. In March 1968, McCarthy came in a close second to Johnson in the New Hampshire primary, gaining 42 percent of the vote. Sensing LBJ's vulnerability, Senator Robert Kennedy of New York joined the fray a week later as a more palatable alternative to Johnson than McCarthy. At the end of March, Johnson announced that he would not seek the nomination.[1]

As McCarthy and Kennedy prepared to slug it out in a handful of primaries across the country, Vice President Hubert Humphrey joined the race in April. Although he entered none of the primaries, he began winning over certain delegations that were being chosen the old fash-ioned way—by party leaders in states that did not tie their convention delegates to the results of primary elections. Then, in June, Robert Kennedy was assassinated in Los Angeles, the day he won the California Democratic primary. By the time of the August convention in Chicago, Humphrey had won over the majority of delegates he needed to clinch the nomination and was far ahead of McCarthy.

The Democratic National Convention exploded in protest. All of the energy and enthusiasm of the party was in the antiwar movement, and an antiwar candidate had won every primary decided by rank-and-file party members. Yet the party was about to nominate LBJ's vice president, who had entered none of the primaries and had won delegates by courting the party bosses, not the people. The turmoil was not confined to the convention hall, as police and protesters skirmished in the streets of Chicago. All in all, the image that the Democratic Party presented to the television audience did not inspire confidence.

In an effort to assuage the activists, the convention agreed to appoint a commission to study the party's presidential nomination process. In 1969, the party established a commission headed by Senators George McGovern of South Dakota and Congressman Don Fraser of Minnesota that was charged with completely overhauling the nomination process to allow greater public participation in the selection of the nominee. The McGovern-Fraser Commission submitted its guidelines for the conduct of the 1972 presidential nominating cycle in 1970, and much of its framework remains the core of the Democratic Party process today.[2] Moreover, since many of its recommendations could only be instituted by changes in state law, the Republican Party has adopted much of the report as well. Thus, those Democratic Party reforms are the foundation of the modern presidential nomination process.

The McGovern-Fraser Commission

The commission's recommendations fell into two general categories. The first involved changes to broaden the pool of potential convention delegates. Each state had established its own rules for choosing convention delegates. Some made the requirements so onerous that the party bosses in effect ended up handpicking the delegates. The report called for efforts to ensure diversity in national convention delegations with respect to race, color, creed, national origin, age, and sex. The report called for relaxed voter registration and a reduction of filing fees and petition requirements. Finally, the report called for transparent rules for the selection of national convention delegates, including the requirement that delegates be chosen in the same year as the election, not the year before.

The second section of the report was designed to strip the state party leaders of the tools they had used to handpick and control their delegations. The rules banned the use of "rump meetings," in which party leaders alone choose the convention delegates. Under the new rules, larger quorums were required and proxy voting was banned for delegate selection. The commission also required that delegations reflect the views of the full range of party members to the greatest extent possible. Delegates were to be selected consistent with the results of primaries or conventions. They were to be apportioned among delegates supporting each of the candidates for president to reflect their level of support in the state, congressional district, or smaller region. Finally, the unit rule, which required all members to vote for the candidate supported by the majority of the state delegation, was forbidden. Thus, individual delegates were free to vote for the candidate of their choice.

The McGovern-Fraser Commission standardized the rules for the selection of delegates to the Democratic National Convention; enforcement of these rules was left to the national party. If a state chose its delegates in a way contrary to party rules, it ran the risk of having the national convention refuse to seat the delegation, thus stripping the state of its influence. Thus, power over the method of choosing delegates shifted from the state party leaders to the national party. Abolishing the unit rule also meant that party bosses lost their primary tool for controlling their delegation once the convention started. However, some aspects of the system remained in the hands of the states. They could choose their delegates either by a primary or a convention. Also, they could pick the date of their nominating contest, so long as it was in the same calendar year as the election. Finally, they retained some flexibility in apportioning delegates among the various candidates.

Conventions and Primaries

The McGovern-Fraser rules gave state parties the option of choosing their delegates to the national convention either by a convention or a primary. The election analyst Rhodes Cook argues that the commission's true preference was for state conventions that open the process up to all party activists but not to the public at large.[3] Nonetheless, primaries became the most popular method employed by states. What is the difference between these two methods and what impact do they have on the ultimate outcome of the process?

A state convention is the final stage of a multitiered process for choosing delegates to the party's national convention. The first step is either a precinct caucus or a local convention. Party members who attend the caucuses or conventions debate party rules, local issues, and planks they would like to see included in the national party platform. During this hours-long meeting, attendees also vote their preferences for presidential nominees. After the votes are tallied, supporters of the various candidates are selected as delegates to the state convention (or perhaps an intermediate-level convention) in the same proportions as in the caucus vote.

Caucuses and conventions tend to attract only party activists because the time and effort involved are quite burdensome. An ordinary voter may be willing to go to a polling place to cast a ballot but not to sit through a three-hour meeting and cast a vote in public. Thus, caucuses are a middle ground between a boss system and a wide-open process. They ensure that the voices of the faithful are all represented, but not those of the unattached voter.

Another unique aspect of the caucus-convention method is that the process continues over many months. Caucuses are used to select delegates for local conventions. Those conventions then choose delegates to attend a state convention where, ultimately, the delegates to the national convention will be chosen. By the final stage of the process, the dynamics of the race may have changed. Some candidates will have dropped out while one candidate may have become the odds-on favorite for the nomination. Thus, the preferences demonstrated in the caucus can easily be overridden by later events. Contests in caucus states are not one-shot deals; the process of building support and momentum continues over many months.

The more popular method for choosing convention delegates is the statewide presidential primary. Primary elections resemble general elections in that voters go to the polls to cast ballots for their preferred candidate but, unlike in general elections in which all registered voters may cast ballots, in most states participation in primary balloting is restricted on the basis of the party registration of the voters. Delegates are then allocated to each of the candidates according to their percentage of the popular vote.

The narrowest form of primary participation occurs in a *closed primary*. In closed primaries, only people who are affiliated with the party via their voter registration are permitted to cast ballots. In an *open primary*, those who are registered as independents may also cast ballots for whichever party they choose. Each state determines by statute which kind of primary it will have.[4] State law also determines how many days in advance (if any) a voter must be registered as a party member in order to participate in its primary. In recent years, several states opted for a wide-open process commonly known as a *blanket primary*. In a blanket primary, the voter is given a single ballot containing the name of all candidates for all parties and all offices. Thus, someone could, for example, vote for a presidential nominee in the Democratic primary and for a candidate for the Senate in the Republican primary.[5] However, the Supreme Court outlawed blanket primaries in June 2000, calling them a violation of a party's right to control its own nomination process.[6]

Does it make any difference for the candidates whether they compete in an open or a closed primary? In general, broader participation favors outsider candidates whereas narrower participation favors candidates with strong organizations and institutional support. A candidate whose message resonates with voters who are not party activists can do well in an open primary because a lot of the votes may be cast by independents. In a caucus or a closed primary in which only the party faithful vote, by contrast, such a candidate would fare poorly. For example, John McCain's early upset victories over George W. Bush in 2000 occurred in open-primary states. Bush crushed McCain in states with closed primaries or caucuses.

What factors influence whether a state chooses to have a caucus or a primary? During the 1970s and '80s, primaries became the more common by far—in 2004, thirty-six of the Democratic state contests were primaries.[7] Cook argues that states initially opted for primaries because they were certain such contests would conform to the guidelines of the McGovern-Fraser Commission. If they held caucuses as a precursor to a state convention, they ran the risk of having their delegation disqualified because the commission rules governing such processes were murkier. Thus, even though McGovern-Fraser sought to encourage conventions, we ended up with primaries instead.[8]

When a party has a contested nomination, there is an added incentive for states to hold a primary. With the exception of Iowa (which gets noticed because of its "first-in-the-nation" status) caucuses draw little attention from candidates. Because turnout is so low, caucus votes are obtained one vote at a time. Candidates cannot invest the time necessary to build up such support, so they have to rely on local organizations. By contrast, primaries generally have higher turnout. Therefore, it makes sense to campaign through the mass media in order to gain the votes of people who are not party activists. A local rally by a candidate will be covered on the local news, spreading the message far beyond the actual attendees to the broad range of people who will show up to vote in the primary.

If there is not a contested presidential nomination, other factors will determine what method a state party uses to select its convention delegates. For example, financial considerations may play a role. In most states, the state government pays the tab for primaries. It must set up polling places and pay poll workers. Since most states hold their presidential primaries much earlier in the year than those for other offices, this is all an additional expense to the state. In the 2004 cycle, a number of states, including Colorado and South Carolina, canceled their presidential primaries, citing a lack of funds owing to rising deficits.[9] Since the state parties had to pay for their own nomination contests, some chose to hold so-called "caucuses," which are much cheaper to run. These caucuses were structured like primaries except that there were a lot fewer polling places around the state and they were open for only a few hours on caucus day. Not only is a caucus and convention cheaper, but conventions can actually be money makers for the parties, since they can collect voluntary admission fees to offset the cost.[10] This provides further incentive for parties to switch to a caucus-convention selection process if there is no particular reason to hold a primary.

Allocating Delegates by State

Both the Republicans and Democrats have followed the McGovern-Fraser Commission's recommendation that the size of a state's delegation to the national convention should reflect the size and strength of its party in the state. The national parties use somewhat different formulas to determine the size of a state's delegation, but both parties take into account a state's population and the party's success at winning elections in the state. The latter criterion consists of bonus delegates for states whose party has won a majority of the congressional delegation, U.S. Senate seats, the governorship, a majority in the state legislature, and the state's electoral votes in the most recent presidential race.

After the 1980 election, the Democratic Party became concerned that the reforms had taken too much power away from party leaders. The nomination contests of 1972, 1976, and 1980 had all been won by party outsiders. In the general elections, McGovern carried only one state, plus the District of Columbia, against President Nixon in 1972; Carter barely defeated a weak, unelected incumbent—President Ford in 1976—and then he lost forty states to Ronald Reagan in 1980. The party feared that the process was generating nominees who would not perform well in November.

In an effort to give party leaders a greater voice, beginning with the 1984 convention the Democrats created a new class of delegates called *superdelegates*, who all were elected officials (U.S. representatives, senators, and governors), members and officers of the Democratic National Committee, and former presidential nominees. These individuals were made automatic delegates to the convention without having to precommit to any particular candidate. Their function has been to act as a delegate bloc that can vote in concert at the convention to ensure that the party chooses a viable presidential nominee. The relative number of superdelegates has made up "roughly 15 to 20 percent of the Democratic convention since 1984," says Cook.[11] In 2004, 801 of the 4,321 delegates to the Democratic National Convention were superdelegates. The Republican Party has never instituted this arrangement.[12]

The "uncommitted" status of superdelegates means that they are not required to back a particular candidate on the first ballot at the convention. Since they were not chosen to reflect the preferences of primary voters, they are allowed to vote their consciences. This does not mean that they have to remain neutral before the convention. Once a superdelegate has determined whom she wishes to support, she is free to announce it. In fact it is in her interest to do so. For example, an Associated Press analysis published on the day of the 2004 Iowa caucuses estimated that 36 percent of superdelegates had already endorsed a candidate. As an elected official, through her support she could enhance the candidate's performance in her state primary. She lends the candidate credibility. She can help him or her with fundraising, voter lists, and other organizational support.

Consequently, the presence of superdelegates means that there are two parallel Democratic campaigns to win convention delegates. About 80 to 85 percent are won through popular election; the rest—the superdelegates—are won through the more informal, insider processes that predominated before McGovern-Fraser. Thus, candidates' success with superdelegates increases the likelihood of victory and, as superdelegates, Democratic Party leaders have been able to reinsert themselves into the nomination process.

Scheduling Primaries and Caucuses

Not surprisingly, in the wake of the McGovern-Fraser reforms, party leaders have sought additional avenues for exercising influence over the presidential nomination process. Professional politicians are not ones to "go gently into that goodnight," as Dylan Thomas memorably put it.

Before McGovern-Fraser, the unit rule and the ability to choose their own loyal convention delegations maximized the influence of state party leaders. Candidates knew that, to win the nomination, they had to cobble together a coalition of state delegations large enough to make a majority. Thus, state party leaders could command concessions from presidential candidates with respect to supporting local economic needs or adopting issue positions necessary to win their state in November. Once the state party leaders made their choice, they could magnify it by guaranteeing the unanimous support of their delegation.

After McGovern-Fraser, with delegates being won through popular election, state party leaders had to find a new way to exercise such influence. After all, they still wanted the presidential nominee to be committed to supporting the local economy. And they still wanted a nominee at the top of the ticket who could win the state and give a boost to the party's candidates farther down the ballot.

The major device they found to obtain leverage over candidates was through the scheduling of their state's nomination contest. The McGovern-Fraser reforms required only that the contest be held in the same year as the general election; precise dates were left up to the individual states. Party leaders saw that if they could schedule their state's primary or caucus at a time to attract the interest of all of the candidates, they could achieve much the same result as they had in the days of the smoke-filled room. Instead of vying for the support of the party boss, the candidates now would compete for the support of the rank-and-file party members—who also wanted a candidate who would support the local economy and would be a viable candidate in November. But how do you schedule your primary to achieve that result?

The simple answer lay in Iowa and New Hampshire. New Hampshire's first-in-the-nation primary had been making headlines since the 1950s. Over the years, it had launched the candidacies of Dwight Eisenhower in 1952 and Barry Goldwater in 1964 while sinking those of Nelson Rockefeller in 1964 and Lyndon Johnson in 1968.[13] Consequently, for years underdog candidates had flocked to New Hampshire in hopes of jump-starting their campaigns, while supporters of the presumptive nominees spent a fortune there to avoid a devastating defeat. The high-stakes drama lured the press, further enhancing New Hampshire's reputation as kingmaker.

Iowa jumped on the bandwagon for the 1972 campaign, albeit for convenience rather than for publicity. The Iowa Democratic Party had traditionally held its state convention in June and wanted to keep it that way. Since the McGovern-Fraser Commission stressed the need for extensive deliberation by party members prior to the opening of a state convention to choose delegates and make platform recommendations, Iowa scheduled its precinct caucuses to take place early, in January. As a presidential candidate, George McGovern knew best how to take advantage of the new rules he had helped craft as the chair of the commission. He devoted the resources necessary to exceed expectations in the Iowa caucuses, and thus catapulted himself to the nomination.[14]

State party leaders learned an important lesson from Iowa and New Hampshire: early contests draw a lot of attention. Candidates knew that an early success could reap major dividends whereas an early defeat could prove fatal. By contrast, states with late primaries would likely get little attention because many candidates already would have dropped out and the eventual nominee would have become apparent. So, in seeking to schedule primaries in a way to attract candidates and exert the most influence on the outcome of the game, state party leaders learned that if you make it early, they will come.

Thus, the new rules created an incentive for state parties to leapfrog over each other to put their primaries and caucuses near the front of the pack. And so they did. Table 2.1 illustrates how much the presidential nomination process has become front-loaded over the years. In both 1976 and 2004, the Iowa caucuses were held on January 19. But very different things happened next. In 1976, candidates had five weeks after Iowa to prepare for the New Hampshire primary, on February 24. Throughout March and April, they faced one or two primaries at a time with one to three weeks separating them. The candidates did not have to campaign in many states simultaneously until May. By contrast, in 2004, New Hampshire followed Iowa by just eight days, and after that, candidates had to compete in multiple primaries nearly every week.

Despite being challenged by other states and the District of Columbia, Iowa and New Hampshire have kept their favored positions at the front of the line. They have done so by codifying their first-in-the-nation status into state law. Section 653.9 of the New Hampshire code establishes the date of the presidential primary: "The presidential primary election shall be held on the second Tuesday in March or on a Tuesday selected by the secretary of state which is 7 days or more immediately preceding the date on which any other state shall hold a similar election, whichever is earlier."

Section 43.4 of Iowa state law provides for the scheduling of the caucuses as follows:

Delegates to county conventions of political parties and party committee members shall be elected at precinct caucuses held not later than the fourth Monday in February of each even-numbered year. The date shall be at least eight days earlier than the scheduled date for any meeting, caucus or primary which constitutes the first determining stage of the presidential nominating process in any other state, territory or any other group which has the authority to select delegates in the presidential nomination.

Thus, Iowa and New Hampshire were able to ensure their privileged positions at the head of the line. If any other state moved ahead of them, Iowa and New Hampshire would automatically reschedule their contests even earlier. Inevitably, as the years went by the primary season kept getting earlier and more intense.

By 2000, the national parties intervened in an effort to limit this front-loading of the primaries. The Republicans awarded bonus delegates to states holding their nomination contests later in the year. However, most states valued having an influential primary more than a few extra delegates, so the plan proved ineffective. The Republicans abandoned the bonus-delegates scheme for the 2004 cycle. The Democratic National Committee voted not to recognize delegations to the 2000 Democratic National Convention from states (other than Iowa and New Hampshire) that held their contests before March 1. This created an imbalance between the two parties; some states held their Republican primaries in February and their Democratic contests later in the year. Consequently, the Republicans dominated the media coverage during the month of February and identified their nominee earlier than the Democrats. In expectation of a hotly contested nomination in 2004, the DNC moved its primary window forward to February 1 so that there would be enough time for the party to unite behind the eventual winner.

Another tactic that states have used to attract the attention of presidential candidates is to have an entire region schedule its contests on the same day, creating a de facto regional primary. The theory is that the candidates would have to demonstrate their compatibility with the political values and economic needs of the region, or risk having another candidate build a massive delegate advantage in a single night. The first such effort occurred in the South on March 9, 1988. After Walter Mondale's forty-nine-state loss in the 1984 presidential election, southern Democrats sought a way to enhance their region's influence so that a more moderate candidate would emerge as the nominee. They decided to create a southern regional primary early in the season that would force the candidates to moderate their issue positions.

As so often happens in politics, the law of unintended consequences undermined the intent of reformers. With a crowded Democratic field in 1988, each campaign focused its efforts on small segments of the southern vote in an effort to win a plurality. The Reverend Jesse Jackson appealed to African-American voters. Governor Michael Dukakis of Massachusetts courted Hispanics and urban white liberals. More conservative southern

TABLE 2.1   Democratic Primaries and Caucuses, 1976 and 2004

	1976 Primaries	2004	
Date	State	State	Primary/ Caucus
January 19	Iowa Caucus	Iowa	Caucus
January 27		New Hampshire	Primary
February 3		Arizona	Primary
		Delaware	Primary
		Missouri	Primary
		New Mexico	Caucus
		North Dakota	Caucus
		Oklahoma	Primary
		South Carolina	Primary
February 7		Michigan	Primary
		Washington	Caucus
February 8		Maine	Caucus
February 10		Tennessee	Primary
		Virginia	Primary
February 14		District of Columbia	Caucus
		Nevada	Caucus
February 17		Wisconsin	Primary
February 24	New Hampshire	Hawaii	Caucus
		Idaho	Caucus
		Utah	Primary
March 2	Massachusetts	California	Primary
	Vermont	Connecticut	Primary
		Georgia	Primary
		Maryland	Primary
		Massachusetts	Primary
		Minnesota	Caucus
		New York	Primary
		Ohio	Primary
		Rhode Island	Primary
		Vermont	Primary
March 8		American Samoa	Caucus
March 9	Florida	Florida	Primary
		Louisiana	Primary
		Mississippi	Primary
		Texas	Primary

(continues)

TABLE 2.1 *(continued)*

Date	1976 Primaries State	2004 State	Primary/ Caucus
March 13		Kansas	Caucus
March 16	Illinois	Illinois	Primary
March 20		Alaska	Caucus
		Wyoming	Caucus
March 23	North Carolina		
April 6	Wisconsin		
April 13		Colorado	Caucus
April 17		North Carolina	Caucus
		Virgin Islands	Caucus
April 24		Guam	Caucus
April 27	Pennsylvania	Pennsylvania	Primary
May 4	Georgia	Indiana	Primary
	Indiana		
	District of Columbia		
May 11	Nebraska	Nebraska	Primary
	West Virginia	West Virginia	Primary
May 18	Maryland	Arkansas	Primary
	Michigan	Kentucky	Primary
		Oregon	Primary
May 25	Arkansas		
	Idaho		
	Kentucky		
	Nevada		
	Oregon		
	Tennessee		
June 1	Montana	Alabama	Primary
	Rhode Island	South Dakota	Primary
	South Dakota		
June 8	California	Montana	Primary
	New Jersey	New Jersey	Primary
	Ohio		

Source: 1976 Schedule: Moore, John L., Jon P. Preimesberger, David R. Tarr, eds. 2001. *Congressional Quarterly's Guide to U.S. Elections, 4th ed, Vol. 1.* Washington DC: CQ Press, pp. 359–364. 2004 Schedule: "2004 Presidential Primaries, Caucuses, and Conventions Chronologically," www.thegreenpapers.com/P04/events.phtml?s=c.

whites split their votes between Senator Al Gore of Tennessee and Congressman Dick Gephardt of Missouri. As a result, the two most liberal candidates in the field, Dukakis and Jackson, got the biggest boost from the South because they did unexpectedly well.

Other regional primaries have been created over the years but none has proved durable. Like the South's in 1988, they have not had the influence over the candidates that their creators desired. Moreover, with so many states on the line in a single day, candidates have targeted their resources where they could get the biggest bang for the buck, and smaller states in the region have not drawn much candidate attention. Since joining a regional primary did not give these states the expected clout, they have tended to opt out in later years. Most of the states' experiments with regional primaries have been a failure.

How, then, can we summarize the development of the presidential nomination calendar in the years since the McGovern-Fraser reforms? First, Iowa and New Hampshire have retained the privilege of being the first two contests, held eight days apart. Most other states have moved their primaries and caucuses around in an effort to attract the attention of the candidates. If they can get the candidates to court their voters, they gain influence over the selection of the nominee. Some of their tactics have involved joining with other states in a regional primary or trying to be the only state holding a contest on a given day.

One overarching trend has been front-loading. It is a virtual certainty that states holding primaries later in the year will have little to no voice in choosing the nominee. By that time, most candidates have dropped out and the winner is already known. Thus, whatever other tactics individual states might apply, the inevitable effect of having the states choose their own primary dates is that the calendar has become earlier and more compact.

As candidates prepare years in advance for a presidential race, they do not know specifically what the calendar will look like. They do not know which states will hold their primaries or caucuses on which day. But they can expect that the general shape of the calendar will look a lot like the one the Democratic candidates faced in 2004, shown in table 2.1. Iowa and New Hampshire stand alone at the front. Because these are small states, candidates must utilize so-called "retail politics"—courting voters one at a time—in order to survive. This means building an extensive grassroots organization in the two states, shaking a lot of hands, and kissing a lot of babies. Once candidates get past that hurdle, they find themselves competing simultaneously in a large number of states spread all across the country. This requires "wholesale politics": paid television advertising and garnering coverage in the news media. Iowa and New Hampshire require time; all the others require money.

Allocating Delegates to Candidates

After all of the votes have been tallied in a primary, we know how much popular support each candidate has. However, presidential nominees are chosen not by how many votes they receive nationwide but by how many national convention delegates vote for them; there is an intermediate step in the process that translates the popular vote into delegate totals. That step is the selection of convention delegates who are committed to voting for a specific candidate on the first ballot at the national convention.

The McGovern-Fraser Commission called for the selection of delegates whose presidential preferences would reflect those of party members in the state. However, it did not establish specific procedures for states to follow. There are two principal methods by which delegates are allocated among the candidates: *winner-take-all* and *proportional representation*. In a winner-take-all scheme, the candidate who receives the most votes wins all of the delegates. Winner-take-all provides the greatest leverage for state party leaders in that it best replicates the old unit rule. Any candidate who wants the support of a state's delegation must campaign hard in the state. It is not enough to do well—you have to win. The winner's reward is that he gets a big boost over his rivals in the delegate count. Another reason why some party leaders support winner-take-all primaries is that they believe it best prepares their candidate for the general election. The electoral vote is winner-take-all by state, so replicating that mechanism in the nomination contests helps train candidates to adopt "winning" strategies, not "vote maximizing" strategies. The downside, of course, is that the delegation's votes do not reflect the relative support in the state for the various candidates.

Under proportional representation, delegates are allocated as accurately as possible according to the percentage of the vote won by the candidates. Under a pure proportional representation system, a candidate who received 10 percent of the vote would get 10 percent of the delegates. However, states seldom adopt pure systems, opting instead for a minimum threshold. Let us assume for a moment that a state adopts a system of proportional allocation of delegates with a 20 percent threshold. After the votes are cast, all candidates who received at least 20 percent of the vote are entitled to receive delegates. The delegates are then allocated among those candidates on the basis of their support relative to each other. For example, suppose that there are three candidates in a primary, who receive 60 percent, 30 percent, and 10 percent of the vote, respectively. The third candidate would get no delegates because he did not reach the 20-percent threshold. The first candidate got twice as many votes as the second, so he would receive two thirds of the delegates and the other would receive one third.

Another option is to split the state into regions (usually congressional districts) for the purpose of allocating convention delegates to candidates. Typically, the state party sets aside a bloc of delegates to be allocated on the basis of the statewide vote, then divides the rest among the congressional districts on the basis of the relative strength of the party in each. Then, statewide delegates will be allotted to candidates on the basis of their statewide performance, and congressional district delegates on the basis of candidates' performance in each congressional district. Either winner-take-all or proportional representation can be used. The latter allows a candidate with appeal in one part of the state to capture delegates even if his statewide support is weak. Either winner-take-all or proportional representation can be used.

The allocation of delegates among candidates is the one area where we find substantial differences between Democrats and Republicans. The scheduling of nomination contests and the rules regarding who is eligible to vote in them are generally determined by state law. Even if laws change from cycle to cycle, whatever rules the state legislature writes apply to both parties. The formulas for establishing the delegation size for each state are similar for the two parties. Both generally are a function of population and party strength. Allocating delegates, however, is purely an internal party matter, and methods of assigning delegates to candidates differ dramatically in the two major parties.

In recent election cycles, the Democratic National Committee has set rules that are nearly universal in application. Virtually all state Democratic parties allocate their delegates using proportional representation with a 15 percent threshold. Some delegates are awarded on the basis of the candidate's performance in each congressional district while others are allotted in accordance with statewide vote totals.

The Republican Party, by contrast, has taken a more laissez-faire approach to how state parties allocate delegates among the candidates. They have issued no rules on the subject, nor have they tried to encourage states one way or the other. As a result, states have adopted widely varying procedures. Table 2.2 shows the number of states adopting the various methods of delegate allocation in 2000.[15] Over half of the states that held a Republican primary for president in 2000 used some form of winner-take-all allocation method. In fourteen states, the candidate winning the most votes got all of the delegates for the state. In eleven states, some of the delegates went to the plurality winner of each congressional district. Of the eighteen other states that held a primary, eleven used proportional representation and seven used some other method. On the Democratic side, thirty-eight states held proportional primaries and eighteen used a convention.

TABLE 2.2   Delegate Allocation Methods, 2000

	Republicans	Democrats
Winner-Take-All—state	14	0
Winner-Take-All—congressional district	11	0
Proportional—congressional district	11	38
Caucus or convention	12	18
Other	7	0

Candidate Strategies

The ultimate goal of the candidates is to win a majority of delegates to the national convention. The rules of the game affect what strategies they will pursue to achieve that goal. Iowa and New Hampshire are fairly straightforward. Voters there expect direct exposure to the candidates on numerous occasions. Because of their small populations, candidates can effectively engage in the retail politics needed to win the voters' support. All it takes is a lot of time and a good organization. Similarly, states that use multitiered caucuses and conventions require constant attention by the candidate's local organization to win support at each point in the process. Beyond that, when candidates have to run in multiple large state primaries at the same time, they must make strategic choices about how best to allocate their time and money. As we have seen, the rules are somewhat different for Democrats and Republicans, and so they adopt different strategies. Let us begin with the Democrats.

Virtually all Democratic primaries allocate delegates by proportional representation with a 15 percent threshold at both the statewide and congressional district levels. In a crowded field, therefore, delegates are likely to be divvied up among several candidates. So long as you reach the 15-percent level in the state and its congressional districts, you will not fall too far behind in any one state. The one way to lose a lot of ground is either to bypass a state or perform very poorly. As the field narrows down to two or three candidates, beating your opponents becomes more important. Since all competitive candidates are likely to meet the minimum threshold, you can gain on your rivals by getting more votes than they do both regionally and statewide. However, you are unlikely to rack up the kind of delegate margins that can be achieved under a winner-take-all system.

Ideally, in a crowded field, a candidate would want to exploit his pockets of strength and survive everywhere else. Suppose, for example, a candidate has a very strong following among a given constituency, such as African Americans or union households. In areas where such voters are highly concentrated, the candidate will win a lot of delegates. In other areas, they could constitute a large enough bloc to win the candidate some delegates. With a crowded field, this will likely be enough to win a few states. Put all this together, and the candidate has had a good night, winning as many delegates as his opponents. As the field narrows, beating your rivals becomes more important. However, it is still quite difficult for candidates who have fallen behind in the cumulative delegate count to make up a lot of ground. The front-runner merely has to win some delegates everywhere to keep his opponents from gaining a lot of ground. Thus, it is vital for Democratic candidates to compete in every state and to develop a broad base of support once the field narrows.

The results of the 2004 Michigan caucuses provide a good illustration of Democratic delegate accumulation strategies in a crowded field. Table 2.3 shows the popular vote percentages and the allocation of Michigan's 128 delegates among the candidates.[16] Senator Kerry performed very well, winning a majority statewide and a plurality in every congressional district. Because his support was both broad and deep, he won 71 percent of the delegates while winning only 52 percent of the popular vote. Governor Dean came in second with 17 percent of the vote, barely clearing the 15-percent threshold for winning statewide delegates. However, Dean got 15 percent or more in only twelve of the fifteen congressional districts. As a result, he won 19 percent of the delegates—somewhat higher than his popular vote total, but not much. Senator Edwards came in third, with 14 percent of the vote, falling just short of what he needed to win statewide delegates. His support was spread fairly evenly across the state and he narrowly crossed the 15 percent threshold in only six congressional districts. Consequently, he won only 6 of Michigan's 128

TABLE 2.3   Michigan Primary Results, 2004

	Percentage of Vote	Delegates Won
Kerry	52	91
Dean	17	24
Edwards	14	6
Sharpton	7	7
Others	10	0

pledged delegates. The Reverend Al Sharpton came in fourth, with only 7 percent of the vote. However, the bulk of his support came from two Detroit districts with high concentrations of African American voters. He narrowly trailed Kerry in those districts and garnered seven delegates. Thus, he was able to accumulate more delegates than Edwards despite getting half as many votes.

Republican delegate allocation among candidates is somewhat different than that for Democrats. Unlike the Democrats, Republican candidates compete in a number of states in which the candidate who gets a plurality of the votes wins all of the delegates. In many other states, some delegates are granted on a winner-take-all basis by congressional district. Consequently, Republicans adopt a different strategy for allocating their campaign resources.

In a pure winner-take-all state, it makes little sense for a candidate to devote resources if he has no chance of winning. Thus, candidates adopt a strategy similar to what they would use in the general election. In November, as the 2000 presidential election so vividly taught us, the candidate who wins the most electoral votes is the one who moves into the White House. Electoral College votes are awarded on a winner-take-all basis, by state.[17] Candidates spend little money in states where they are sure winners or losers; instead, to maximize their electoral votes, they pour all of their funds into competitive states.

Whereas the Democratic Party mechanism rewards breadth of support in a close nomination contest, the Republican Party mechanism rewards effective targeting. Close doesn't count—you must win states and congressional districts. This also means that delegate allocation in Republican primaries can be wildly disproportionate to the relative level of support among the candidates; someone who wins just 51 percent of the vote gets 100 percent of the delegates. A candidate who wins a number of early states can open up an enormous lead in the delegate count. Similarly, a candidate who is trailing the field can get back in the game quickly by winning a few winner-take-all states.

Summary

The McGovern-Fraser Commission reforms of the presidential nominating process were designed to democratize the process by shifting power from party leaders to party members. However, the federal structure of the United States government made it impossible for the commission to establish a single national system. States are responsible for their own elections—especially for how nomination contests are held. Consequently, the power to decide how presidential candidates were to be nominated ended up in many hands—not just those of party members but also those of national and state party leaders. Once again, the law of unintended consequences was in effect, ensuring that the system that ultimately evolved would be very different from the one envisioned by the commission. Too many cooks spoiled the broth.

All power could not be taken away from state party leaders. Federalism guaranteed that they would have a great deal of latitude in deciding how convention delegates would be chosen from their states. The McGovern-Fraser rules created broad guidelines but the state parties were allowed to fill in the gaps. Of course, they used this flexibility to enhance their own state's influence over the process. Since they could no longer command loyalty from convention delegates to gain leverage over the candidates, they used their scheduling power to get the candidates to court the state's voters. But candidates would only take notice of a state's contest if it took place before the identity of the nominee was apparent. States began leapfrogging over each other to get to the front of the pack. Iowa and New Hampshire have maintained their privileged position at the front of the line, but they are immediately followed by a pack of states all holding their primaries at about the same time. The campaign season has been dramatically front-loaded.

The Democratic National Committee has attempted to step in to regulate this process, but has had only limited success. The one tool that the DNC has to enforce its will is refusing to seat convention delegations that were chosen in ways it did not condone. The DNC has tried to put a brake on front-loading by setting a date before which no state other than Iowa and New Hampshire would be allowed to choose delegates. Succumbing to reality, however, the DNC has moved that date all the way forward to February 1. Similarly, it has required all but a few states to allocate their delegates among candidates using a system of proportional representation by congressional district. The Republican Party's philosophy toward the presidential nomination process has been consistent with its historical preferences on economic policy—laissez faire. The Republicans have taken few actions to regulate how states choose their delegations. As a result, many states use a winner-take-all system for their Republican primaries.

As the system has evolved, so have the candidates' strategies. The front-loading of the primary season has limited a candidate's ability to build a campaign from scratch in later states once the primary season is under way. There are just too many races and too little time. Preparation and momentum become all-important. Consequently, candidates focus their resources on the early state contests but must develop strength in later states as well. This is particularly important for Democrats because the proportional allocation of delegates places a premium on geographic breadth of support. With winner-take-all primaries, a Republican candidate can target some states while ignoring others without harming his ability to accumulate delegates. The bottom line for candidates of both parties is that the front-loaded nomination system forces them to build support for their campaign in the year before Iowa—nearly two years before the general election.

Delegate selection rules were not the only part of the presidential nomination process that was overhauled in the 1970s. Four years after the McGovern-Fraser Commission completed its work, Congress overhauled the campaign finance system. Fundraising and spending for presidential campaigns became subject to regulation and limitation. This, too, dramatically affected the nomination process in a way that amplified the effects of the front-loaded schedule.

Notes

1. Johnson never formally joined the race for reelection. He did not enter the New Hampshire primary but received 48 percent of the vote as a write-in candidate.

2. The full text of the McGovern-Fraser Commission recommendations can be found in Nelson W. Polsby, *Consequences of Party Reform* (Oxford, England: Oxford University Press, 1983), pp. 40–52.

3. Rhodes Cook, *The Presidential Nominating Process: A Place for Us?* (Lanham, Md.: Rowman & Littlefield, 2003), pp. 44–46.

4. Some states do not register voters by party. In those states, a party, before letting voters cast a ballot in its primary, often requires them to sign a pledge saying that they intend to support the party's nominee in the general election. Since such pledges are unenforceable, parties in such states have virtually no control over who votes in their primaries.

5. Such a system was in place for the California presidential primary in 2000. To avoid having Democrats cross over to vote in the Republican primary, the Republican National Committee announced that it would not recognize convention delegations chosen by blanket primaries. This led California to keep separate tallies of the primary votes, one of all votes cast for Republican presidential candidates and one of votes cast by registered Republicans only. The latter was used to select the convention delegates.

6. *California Democratic Party vs. Jones*, 530 U.S. 567 (2000).

7. The Democratic and Republican parties hold fifty-five nominating contests—one for each state, and for American Samoa, the District of Columbia, Guam, Puerto Rico, and the Virgin Islands. Democrats also elect a convention delegation to represent Democrats living abroad.

8. Cook, *Presidential Nominating Process*, pp. 44–46.

9. Most of these states' legislatures were controlled by Republicans. Since there weren't any challengers for the Republican presidential nomination, little need was seen for a primary.

10. The Supreme Court outlawed mandatory admission fees to state party conventions that nominate candidates, finding that such fees were tantamount to a poll tax. See *Morse v. Virginia Republican Party*, 517 U.S. 186 (1996).

11. Cook, *Presidential Nominating Process*, pp. 56–58.

12. The Democratic National Committee has much more authority to change its nomination rules than does the Republican National Committee. At each national convention, Republicans set the rules for the nomination process four years later; the RNC is not empowered to make changes independently in the intervening time. By contrast, the Democratic National Committee can vote to change the nominating rules on its own authority. Consequently, the Democrats have shown a much greater tendency to adjust their procedures from one election cycle to another.

13. For a thorough history of the New Hampshire primary from 1952 through 1984, see Charles Brereton, *First in the Nation: New Hampshire and the Premier Presidential Primary* (Portsmouth, N.H.: Peter E. Randall, 1987).

14. David Yepsen, "Iowa's Caucuses: An Introduction and History," *Des Moines Register* website, DesMoinesRegister.com/extras/politics/caucus2004/history.html.

15. Data from the 2000 presidential contests were used to compare the practices of the two parties because it was the last cycle in which both parties had a contested nomination.

16. Data on the rules for state party nomination contests in 2000 and 2004 were compiled from data available on-line at www.thegreenpapers.com.

17. The two exceptions to this rule are Maine and Nebraska, which allot some of their electoral votes on a winner-take-all basis by congressional district.

3

The Formal Rules—
Campaign Finance

T H E   V I O L E N C E   A T   T H E   1968 Democratic National Convention was not the only event of that turbulent political era that fundamentally changed how parties select their presidential nominees. The uncovering of the Watergate scandal between 1972 and 1974 exposed the dark underbelly of how federal campaigns were financed. A staple of political campaigns had been unmarked envelopes filled with thousands of dollars in cash to be handed, discreetly, to candidates' "surrogates"— colleagues, friends, campaign workers, and so on. But the volume of such undisclosed contributions to the Nixon presidential campaign and their use to fill up a slush fund used as hush money for the Watergate burglars made the continuation of such a system untenable.

In 1974, Congress passed and President Ford signed into law legislation amending the Federal Elections Campaign Act (FECA) of 1971, which had strengthened contribution disclosure rules and taken steps to slow the rising cost of campaigns. These amendments completely overhauled the way in which elections for Congress and the presidency were to be financed. Although the Supreme Court overturned large portions of the legislation relating to congressional campaigns in its 1976 ruling in *Buckley v. Valeo*, it left the presidential system intact.[1] Thus, FECA remains the law that governs how presidential campaigns are financed.

The FECA presidential system contains four pillars: contribution limits, public disclosure, spending limits, and public financing. The contribution limits are mandatory but the spending limits and public financing are voluntary. This chapter details each of these, describing both the formal rules of the game and the techniques that campaigns use to bend the rules in their favor. We then outline how the political parties and interest groups use their own money to affect presidential nominations outside the formal channels established in FECA. Finally, we examine the impact of the Bipartisan Campaign Reform Act (BCRA) of 2002 on the rules for financing presidential nominations and assess whether future campaigns will continue to abide by the voluntary provisions of the law.

Contribution Limits

In *Buckley v. Valeo*, the Supreme Court equated money with speech, and it found all mandatory limitations except one to be violations of the First Amendment. The Court did, however, uphold the limitation on individual contributions made directly to campaigns. The Court viewed money contributed directly to campaigns as falling under the rubric of free association, not free speech, and on this basis it upheld such limitations contained in FECA on the amount of money an individual could legally contribute to a campaign. These regulated direct contributions are known as "hard money."

During the presidential campaigns from 1976 through 2000, individuals were limited to $1,000 in contributions to any candidate for federal office during an election cycle (raised to $2,000 in 2002), which for presidential candidates covers the entire nomination campaign. Of course, there were loopholes that allowed this figure to be inflated; for example, a married couple could both give $1,000 to a presidential candidate, and it has not been uncommon for people to contribute from the accounts of their minor children as well despite regulations to limit such abuses. The loophole does not extend, however, beyond the family unit. Many of the convictions and guilty pleas for campaign finance violations during the 1996 presidential election resulted from people laundering donations through their friends or business associates.

Political action committees (PACs) are another source of hard money available to presidential candidates. In order to increase the clout of small donors who cannot afford to give the maximum individual contribution, Congress allowed the formation of PACs, which are entitled to give up to $5,000 to a candidate. The theory is that PACs enable small donors to pool their resources. A $50 contribution from a small donor would be unnoticed by a campaign receiving many $2,000 checks, but if one hundred like-minded people came together to make a $5,000 PAC donation, the campaign would notice. To qualify as a legal PAC, the organization must collect money from at least fifty-one individuals and donate to at least five federal campaigns in each election cycle.

The campaigns themselves are required to monitor the money they receive to ensure that they do not accept any beyond what is allowed by law. Under the public disclosure provisions of FECA, they are required to report all contributions of $200 or more to the Federal Election Commission (FEC), which compiles the information and publicly discloses it.[2] For presidential campaigns, the collection and disclosure requirements begin as soon as a candidate either officially announces that she is running or forms an "exploratory committee." An exploratory committee allows the candidate to collect money and spend it for the purpose of gauging support for the race. As a practical matter, announcing the creation of an exploratory committee is no different from announcing one's candidacy as far as campaign finance laws are concerned.

Spending Limits

The FECA amendments of 1974 established mandatory limits for congressional races and voluntary ones for presidential races. In 1976, the Supreme Court in *Buckley v. Valeo* overturned the mandatory spending limits for congressional campaigns but allowed voluntary limits for presidential races. To encourage presidential candidates to voluntarily limit their spending, FECA established partial public financing for primary campaigns and full public financing for the general election. Presidential candidates may opt out of the spending limits system—but if they do so they forego receiving campaign funds from the federal treasury.

The 1974 amendments to FECA capped the total amount that a candidate may spend in pursuit of the presidential nomination at $10 million. Congress indexed that figure to account for inflation; also, 20 percent of a campaign's expenses—the amount assumed to cover fundraising costs—is exempt from the limits. Thus, for the 2004 contest, the FEC estimates that the effective spending limit for a presidential candidate rose to $44.6 million. FEC regulations also permit campaigns to spend additional money on accounting and legal expenses required to comply with the law.

Since the quest for delegates is really a series of statewide contests, Congress also placed limits on how much money candidates who accept federal funding can spend in each state. These limits, adjusted each cycle for inflation, are fixed as a percentage of the voting age population.

However, the formula for calculating each state's limit is such that the sum of all the state limits is much greater than the nationwide limit. Candidates therefore have to ration their money so that they spend it as strategically as possible within the bounds of the nationwide spending limit.

Not surprisingly, presidential campaigns have found ways to bend the limits for individual states so that they can maximize their spending in key states. For example, ABC is the only broadcast network with an affiliate in New Hampshire that reaches the population centers of Manchester and Nashua. The other networks serve that market from Boston. If a campaign purchases ads on a Boston television station, only a small percentage of that spending will count toward the New Hampshire limit and the balance will apply to Massachusetts. In this way, some of a campaign's Massachusetts spending supplements its New Hampshire spending, thereby stretching the candidate's exposure in that key early primary state. Similarly, a candidate campaigning in western Iowa could spend the night across the river in Omaha, Nebraska, in order to put hotel and other expenses on the Nebraska instead of the Iowa account, freeing up some more Iowa funds. Nonetheless, all of that spending counts toward the national limit, so every extra dollar used to influence one state is a dollar that cannot be used elsewhere.

For years, no candidate who rejected spending limits made a serious impact on a presidential nomination contest. In 1980, John Connally, the Republican former governor of Texas, opted out of the spending-limits system and raised over $10 million for his campaign, but he won only a single convention delegate. Steve Forbes, in 1996, was the first candidate who opted out of the system and made some impact: in his pursuit of the Republican nomination, Forbes accumulated $41.7 million—$37.5 million from his own bank account—and spent heavily in several early primary states. He won the Delaware and Arizona primaries but lost the nomination to Senator Bob Dole of Kansas. As a candidate in 2000, Forbes again chose to reject spending limits and public financing. Not wanting to be outspent, then Governor George W. Bush of Texas opted out of the system as well. Forbes raised $48.1 million, of which $42.3 million came from his own pocket. Bush raised $94.5 million, all from outside contributors. Bush went on to win the nomination handily, and Forbes did not win a single contest.

For the 2004 cycle, Bush again opted out of the spending limits system during the primary season. He smashed his previous record by raising more than $240 million through July 2004 in his uncontested quest for his party's nomination. On the Democratic side, Senator John Kerry of Massachusetts and the former Vermont governor Howard Dean decided to opt out as well because they feared being massively outspent by Bush prior to the summer national conventions, which mark the formal end of the nominating season.

Public Financing

An important source of funding for most presidential nomination contestants is the system of partial public financing. In order to be eligible for funding from the U.S. Treasury, a candidate must first demonstrate a certain breadth of support. This entails raising at least $5,000 in contributions of up to $250 in each of at least twenty states. Once this requirement is met, the government considers the candidacy to be viable enough to be worthy of public financing.

At that point, a campaign becomes eligible for matching funds. The U.S. Treasury matches the first $250 of every individual contribution that the candidate receives. This continues until the campaign has raised enough money to meet the overall spending limit—$45 million in 2004. The Treasury cannot begin releasing the funds until January of the election year, which has become problematic for campaigns as a result of the front-loading of the primaries and the need to spend a lot of money before January. To solve this problem, candidates can borrow money using anticipated matching funds as collateral. Lenders know for certain that the money will be coming so they are willing to make the loans. Thus, campaigns are able to utilize matching funds long before they actually receive them.

Candidates become ineligible for matching funds if they withdraw from the race or if it becomes obvious that their candidacy is no longer viable—namely, when a candidate receives less than 5 percent of the vote in two successive contested primaries. Thus, if a candidate is trying to focus his resources only on states in which he believes he can do well, the campaign will let it be known that the candidate is not running in other states, and then these states will not count for the viability requirement.

If a campaign loses matching funds due to nonviability, it can become eligible again if it receives at least 20 percent of the vote in a primary in another state. Once a candidate decides that he cannot win the nomination and withdraws from the race, he or she forfeits any matching funds not yet delivered. Thus, candidates often announce that they are "suspending campaign activity" rather than "withdrawing from the race."

The U.S. Treasury draws the matching funds from the Presidential Election Campaign Fund, which is funded by taxpayers who check off a box on their income tax forms to channel money into the account. The Federal Election Campaign Act amendments of 1974 allowed taxpayers to dedicate one dollar of their federal income taxes for this purpose. In 1993 the amount was raised to three dollars. In recent cycles, there has been a great deal of concern that there would not be enough money in the pot to provide all of the matching funds to which the candidates were entitled. As spending limits rise with every cycle, so rises the need for matching funds. Furthermore, fewer taxpayers are checking the box on their returns to put money into the fund. The Campaign Finance Institute, a private research organization, notes that the percentage of taxpayers contributing to the fund has declined from a high of 25.7 percent in 1981 to around 11 percent in recent years.[3] The only reason there was enough money to fully meet all matching fund requests in 2000, when both parties had contested nominations, and in 2004, when the Democrats had nine candidates, was that a number of candidates opted out of the public financing and spending limits system. The institute projects that if all candidates for the 2004 nomination from both parties had sought public financing, the fund would have been $20 million short.[4]

The Democratic and Republican candidates who win their party's nomination face a different system of public financing for the general election. Each may opt for full public financing in exchange for raising no private contributions for the campaign. Thus, if both nominees accept public funding, they each receive an identical amount for the general election. Because the funding level is indexed to inflation, the total amount of public funds given to each of the two main candidates in 2004 was $75 million. Other candidates are eligible for full public funding only if their party received at least 25 percent of the popular vote in the previous presidential election. They can receive a lesser amount if the party won at least 5 percent of the popular vote. The only other party to achieve this status was the Reform Party, whose 2000 nominee was eligible for $12.6 million in public funding as a result of Ross Perot's winning 9 percent of the vote in 1996[5]. The $12.6 million served as a magnet that attracted everyone from Pat Buchanan on the far right to Lenora Fulani on the far left to compete for the Reform Party nomination.[6] No major party nominee has rejected public funding for the general election since the system was established in 1974.

Conventions' Effect on Election Finances

The timing of the general election funding can have an impact on the nomination process. Candidates do not receive the money until they are officially nominated at the party convention. This event usually occurs in July or August of the election year, although the 2004 Republican National Convention concluded in September. Consequently, candidates have to make sure their campaign money lasts until their party's convention so that there is no significant period of silence, which could prove fatal for a candidacy.

In 2004, the timing of the Democratic and Republican national conventions had a further effect on spending for the general election. Traditionally, the party that controls the White House holds its convention later than the challenging party. After the Democrats scheduled their convention for the last week in July, the Republicans opted for the week before Labor Day—the latest date that a national nominating convention had ever been held. This meant that John Kerry, the Democratic nominee, had to make his $75 million general election account last five weeks longer than did President Bush. To overcome this disadvantage, Kerry briefly toyed with the idea of delaying his formal acceptance of the nomination until September, but he abandoned the plan when it elicited widespread criticism.

Party Soft Money

The system by which hard money flows directly into and out of presidential campaigns is a highly regulated one. It consists of limited contributions, regulated spending, and some degree of public financing. How does this square with the avalanche of news stories on big contributors giving hundreds of thousands of dollars at a pop to politicians? How can this happen? Beyond the regulated world of hard money lies the "soft-money" sector, the Wild West of campaign finance.

After the FECA amendments of 1974, Congress became concerned that parties might no longer be able to play a significant role in elections. Political parties had traditionally provided the money and manpower for grassroots politics. If party contributions operated under the same rules as individual contributions, Congress feared that grassroots citizen activism would decay. Consequently, in 1979, Congress further amended FECA to allow political parties to spend unlimited amounts for "party-building activities."

This exception exacerbated what was already a rather tricky situation. The U.S. Constitution gives the states great latitude in regulating their own elections. Thus, while Congress could pass laws regulating campaigns for national offices, it could not do so for state and local elections. Each state is allowed to establish its own rules for state and local political activities, and most of them have far looser restrictions, particularly with respect to contribution limits, than the federal government. Complicating the picture is the fact that political parties are vertically integrated, so activities that help the national party also help the local parties and vice versa. Consequently, money raised by parties becomes like a giant witches' brew: though some is raised under federal law and some under fifty different state laws, when it is spent it helps party organizations at all levels.

In an effort to limit the effect of soft money on federal elections, the Federal Election Commission, in a series of opinions between 1976 and 1978, allowed the parties to maintain dual accounts: one for hard money and one for soft money. Expenditures were to be drawn from the two accounts in proportion to the relative impact of the spending on national and state elections. In spite of this effort, the combination of unlimited contributions to parties under state laws and unlimited expenditures by national parties created what became a large and lightly regulated alternative system by which money can affect elections.

Since soft money is designed to assist parties, not candidates, there are two major limitations on its use. First of all, it cannot be given directly to candidates running for federal office, since that would constitute a campaign contribution instead of an expenditure for "party building." Second, the national parties are not permitted to coordinate their spending activities with the campaigns, since doing so would represent a backdoor contribution—if a candidate's campaign organization instructs the party how to spend money, that is in effect no different from the party giving money for the campaign to spend as it sees fit. Thus, soft money is limited to "party-building activities" that are not "coordinated" with the campaign. Yet, these two words are vague enough so that they open the door wide to a great deal of mischief.

What exactly is a "party-building activity"? Does it include door-to-door canvassing? What about lawn signs? Or bumper stickers? Or get-out-the-vote calls? All of these are vital grassroots activities of the kind Congress sought to encourage, but they also have a significant impact on individual election campaigns. What about a national television advertising campaign extolling the virtues of a party? What if it also criticizes the other party? What if it criticizes the presidential candidate from one party and encourages people to vote for the other party? These are clearly not grassroots organizing efforts, yet they are designed to mobilize the party faithful and encourage others to join. As the law has been interpreted over the years, almost any party activity could be structured to fit within the definition of party building. Consequently, over time the restrictions on the use of soft money have become relatively meaningless as the parties have found ways to circumvent them.

Exactly what does "coordination" mean? Suppose a campaign runs ads attacking the opposition on a particular issue and the party begins to run its own commercials on the same subject without consulting the campaign. Is this a coordinated activity? Suppose the party decides to spend money to canvass key precincts in a hotly contested area. It tells the candidate it is doing so but does not ask permission. The candidate knows, therefore, that his campaign does not need to duplicate that effort. Is this a coordinated activity? Over the years, campaign professionals have been able to structure their activities to avoid having their efforts fall under the definition of coordination. Thus, over the years the national parties have found ways around all soft-money restrictions.

What impact does a party's soft money have on the presidential nomination process? One practical point is that since the parties feel the need to remain neutral in the nomination contest, they do not spend soft money in an effort to determine the nominee. In spite of this self-restrictive stance, there are two ways a party can use its soft money to assist its candidates before the outcome is known. First of all, the party can use its money to attack the other party's likely nominee. In the give and take of the nomination battle, the candidates will be focusing more on each other than on the candidate they may face in November. The national party can pick up the slack by attacking the opposition until the nomination is decided. Second, the party can provide a financial cushion to its candidates as they bump up against the spending limit months before one candidate is nominated and receives public money for the general election. Although the candidates may not be able to spend money, the party can. This eases the burden caused by having presidential primaries and caucuses take place many months before the convention.

Independent Expenditures

The fourth leg of the campaign finance stool is generally called *independent expenditures*. This includes money that is spent by individuals or groups, not by campaigns or parties. It is currently the least regulated of all forms of political spending. In *Buckley v. Valeo*, the Supreme Court ruled that individuals and groups have a First Amendment right to spend their own money for political purposes without regulation. In short, money is speech and is unlimited as long as it does not cross the line separating spending as political speech from de facto campaign contributions.

The most direct form of independent expenditure occurs when the candidate spends his or her own money on the campaign. In *Buckley v. Valeo*, the Court found that this was a clear example of free speech rights that could not be forcibly abridged by the government. Consequently, candidates have the right to spend as much of their own money on their campaigns as they wish.

Nonetheless, the presidential campaign finance system does in fact place restrictions on this kind of spending. Any candidate opting to accept public funds also must agree to limit personal contributions to the campaign. In return for public money, candidates must agree not only to limit their aggregate fundraising and spending but also to contribute no more than $50,000 of their personal funds to the effort. If a candidate chooses to opt out of the public funding system, he can spend as much as he wants. For example, Steve Forbes contributed $37.5 million to his unsuccessful 1996 presidential campaign.

The second form of independent expenditures occurs when individuals or groups outside of the campaign and the party spend money on political activity that affects the race. For example, an interest group may run television ads highlighting a particular issue and noting the positions of candidates or parties. Similarly, groups often distribute voter guides that detail the positions of the candidates in an election on issues of concern to the group. The Supreme Court has ruled that such activities are a form of political speech that is protected by the First Amendment.

As with soft money, however, there are limits on independent expenditures. They cannot be coordinated with the campaign or be used as de facto contributions in any other way. The standard for judging whether political activities are coordinated with the campaign is quite murky. For example, in his 1988 presidential campaign against Governor Michael Dukakis of Massachusetts, Vice President Bush's campaign ran an ad highlighting the Massachusetts prison furlough system, under which prisoners serving life sentences were given weekend furloughs. One such prisoner, Willie Horton, raped and murdered a woman while on one of these weekend passes. The video on the Bush ad showed a revolving door on a prison with convicts cycling through it while an announcer told the story of Willie Horton. The purpose of the Bush ad was to depict Dukakis as soft on criminals. Soon thereafter, an outside group calling itself the National Security Political Action Committee ran its own ad on the subject using its own money. NSPAC's notorious version showed a menacing picture of Willie Horton, an African American, shrouded in shadows while the announcer recounted Horton's crimes. Although NSPAC did not coordinate the ad with the Bush campaign, it reiterated one of the campaign's messages in a more dramatic and memorable fashion. Nonetheless, NSPAC's ad was considered to be an uncoordinated independent expenditure.

Rulings by the Supreme Court and the Federal Election Commission have helped to define the line between an independent expenditure and a campaign contribution. Essentially, as long as an ad does not specifically endorse or reject a candidate for office, it is considered "issue advocacy," and is not subject to campaign contribution limits. If the ad uses so-called "magic words" such as "vote for" or "vote against," it is deemed "express advocacy" and counts as a campaign contribution subject to limitation. Not unexpectedly, however, interest groups have figured out numerous clever ways to make it perfectly clear which candidate they support without using the magic words. For example, a radio ad might excoriate an office holder for a vote she cast or an issue position she has taken. But the ad's tag line will be "Call Senator Jones and tell her how upset you are," not "Vote Senator Jones out of office." In this way, the interest group can express its strong opposition to Senator Jones while maintaining its unregulated status.

Campaign Finance Reform

The system for financing American elections has developed over the years into one with two parallel tracks. On one track, the core system, contributions are strictly limited. In presidential campaigns, this track offers the option of spending limits and partial public financing. The other track is that of soft money and independent expenditures with no restraints on either contributions or spending. The growing concern about the effects big money contributions were having on elections—both the size of the contributions themselves and the necessity for such massive amounts of money because of the spiraling costs of running an effective campaign—finally led to the enactment of campaign finance reform.

In 2002, Congress passed and President George W. Bush signed into law the Bipartisan Campaign Reform Act (BCRA). The road to its enactment had been long and tortuous. The first serious efforts after the FECA amendments of 1974 to reform campaign finance law began in the mid-1980s. "Efforts to reform the campaign finance system in the 1980s and into the 1990s," write Diane Dwyre and Victoria Farrar-Myers, "focused primarily on the influence of PACs and special interests, the growing cost of congressional elections, and the financial advantages of incumbents."[7] All such efforts were blocked by Senate Republicans, generally by means of filibusters to talk the bill to death.

After a series of campaign finance scandals surrounding the 1996 presidential election erupted, the emphasis changed. Instead of limiting PACs, reformers focused on what Dwyre and Farrar-Myers call the "twin evils" of soft money and independent expenditures.[8] During the 1996 campaigns, soft money and independent expenditures dwarfed the hard-money system for both presidential and congressional campaigns. Unregulated money had replaced regulated money as the predominant currency of federal elections.

Senator John McCain's 2000 presidential race was the galvanizing event that led to the eventual success of campaign finance reform. Since 1995, McCain and his Democratic colleague Senator Russ Feingold of Wisconsin had been crafting bills that served as the primary legislative vehicles for reformers. McCain placed the issue at the top of the agenda of his presidential candidacy and used it to excite thousands of independent voters. When the Senate reconvened in 2001, a number of Republican senators who had previously assisted in blocking reform signed onto McCain-Feingold, making a filibuster impossible. In 2002, the Bipartisan Campaign Reform Act (BCRA), which combined the McCain-Feingold proposals with a similar House bill sponsored by Congressmen Christopher Shays, a Connecticut Republican, and Marty Meehan, a Massachusetts Democrat, passed in both chambers and was signed by President Bush.

Table 3.1 summarizes the major changes BCRA made in campaign finance rules as they pertain to presidential nominations. The principal goal of BCRA was to eliminate soft money and rein in independent expenditures, thereby reinforcing the hard-money system. An additional goal of these measures was to decrease the amount of money spent on elections—which appealed to some reformers. The legislation eliminated soft money at the federal level by forbidding national parties and federal office holders from raising it. From now on, each national party organization could collect no more than $25,000 from any contributor in a given year. BCRA sought to close the loophole whereby state party soft money was used for organizational efforts that benefited federal campaigns by allowing such activities only up to 120 days before a federal election; after that they would be treated as federal activities subject to federal regulation. In short, during the final phase of an election in which federal offices were on the ballot, state parties could only use hard money.

BCRA also defined a new, more restrictive line between unregulated "issue advocacy," which independent organizations may undertake, and

TABLE 3.1   Selected Campaign Finance Rules Governing Presidential Nomination

	Before BCRA	After BCRA
Campaign spending	• National limit of $45 million (for 2004) • Statewide sublimits • Public match on contributions up to $250 *OR* • No spending limits and no public financing	• National limit of $45 million (for 2004) • Statewide sublimits • Public match on contributions up to $250 *OR* • No spending limits and no public financing
Individual contributions (hard money)	• $1,000 per person per campaign • $5,000 per PAC per campaign • Unlimited contributions to parties • Unlimited contributions to own campaign	• $2,000 per person per campaign • $5,000 per PAC per campaign • $25,000 limit on contributions to a national party committee per person per year • Unlimited contributions to own campaign
Party spending	• Derived from unlimited contributions (soft money) • Used for "party-building activities" • Not coordinated with campaign	• Derived from limited contributions (hard money) • Tighter definition of "party-building activities" • Not coordinated with campaign
Independent expenditures	• Unlimited for own campaign • Confined to "issue advocacy" • Derived from unlimited contributions (soft money) • Not coordinated with campaign	• Unlimited for own campaign • Tighter definition of "issue advocacy" • Derived from unlimited contributions up to thirty days before primary (soft money); derived from limited contributions within thirty days of primary (hard money) • Not coordinated with campaign

regulated "express advocacy," which had to be funded with hard money. Any activities by outside groups occurring within thirty days of a primary election and sixty days of a general election for federal office were determined to have an electoral impact. Consequently, all such expenditures would constitute "express advocacy," which must be paid for with hard money. BCRA did not eliminate independent expenditures but subjected them to the same contribution limits that campaigns face. The drafters of BCRA were unable to find a constitutional way to limit self-financing by wealthy candidates. For Senate races they opted instead to increase the contribution limit for candidates whose opponents make large contributions to their own campaigns; they added no such provision for House candidates.

In the final negotiations leading up to the passage of the Bipartisan Campaign Reform Act, some potential supporters voiced concerns that the hard-money system needed to be bolstered. Some thought that the $1,000 contribution limit made it too difficult to raise the immense amount of money required to run an effective campaign in the television age. Consequently, BCRA raised the limit to $2,000 per contributor per race—primary or general election—and indexed that figure to inflation. Moreover, it raised the amount of hard money an individual can contribute to political parties and political action committees to a combined total of $57,500 per two-year election cycle, indexed to inflation. However, it kept the limit that PACs could contribute at $5,000 to candidates and $15,000 to national parties per election cycle.

Anticipating that the law's constitutionality would be challenged immediately, the drafters provided for expedited judicial review. In December 2003, the Supreme Court, in *McConnell v. FEC*,[9] upheld the constitutionality of BCRA and eliminated only a few minor provisions of the law, keeping its basic structure intact.

What impact does BCRA have on the strategies of the candidates and party leaders? The law was designed primarily to affect congressional races and did not change the fundamental structure of the presidential campaign finance system. Nevertheless, John Green and Anthony Corrado have noted both direct and indirect effects of BCRA on candidates seeking their party's presidential nomination. The increase in the contribution limit for individuals from $1,000 to $2,000 has made it easier for candidates to raise more money faster. Green and Corrado also note an indirect effect of this provision. BCRA did not change the $250 threshold up to which the U.S. Treasury matches contributions, and so the importance of public money has decreased relative to that of private donations. Candidates now have an easier time raising the maximum amount allowed under spending limitations and are less likely to need the public money. Green and Corrado argue that campaigns will be more likely than previously to expend more fundraising effort on obtaining large donations, since a $2,000 individual contribution is worth much more than the $500 resulting from a $250 gift and the maximum federal match.[10]

The other major impact of BCRA on the financing of presidential campaigns comes from the soft-money ban. In the past, the national party could use soft money to support a nominee who came out of a competitive primary season having spent the maximum allowed by law. The party could make sure that its apparent nominee could maintain a visible campaign in the long months leading up to the convention. Under BCRA, the parties would be limited to using hard money for this endeavor. Because of this, Democratic National Committee Chairman Terry McAuliffe created a hard-money account to be used for that specific purpose. His goal was to raise $100 million to support the party's nominee. Even if successful, this total represents a substantial drop from the $261 million raised by the DNC in the 2000 election cycle, according to data from the Federal Election Commission. Consequently, BCRA has made it even more important for the party to settle on a nominee before resources are exhausted.

527 Committees

Efforts to regulate political spending are sometimes likened to squeezing a balloon: when you restrict it in one place it expands in another. It comes as no surprise, then, that soft money has found a way back into political campaigns. In the aftermath of BCRA, organizations known as 527 committees, named after the section of the tax code under which they are formed, have flourished. These groups are independent political organizations that are not limited in their fundraising by the $2,000-per-person contribution limit. They use soft money for advertising, grassroots organizing, and many other political activities usually performed by political parties. However, they are not allowed to coordinate their activities with campaigns, cannot engage in "express advocacy," and cannot spend soft money within thirty days of an election. Though nominally independent, they usually are managed by political professionals who have long histories of activism in one of the parties. In effect, they act as "shadow parties." Thus, BCRA did not really eliminate soft money, it merely privatized it.

Should a Candidate Accept Public Financing?

Every candidate seeking his party's nomination for President chooses which financing system to use. He can spend as much as he wants if he chooses not to accept partial public funding, but if he accepts public money he must agree to national and statewide spending limits. Which choice makes the most sense for a candidate? The decision is complicated by the fact that the quest for the presidency is a two-stage process. A candidate has to be nominated by his party before he can run in the general election. The option that enhances the chances of winning the general election may disadvantage the candidate's attempt to win the nomination. The proper selection depends on several factors facing the candidate.

Perhaps the best way to explore the options is to examine the cases of John Kerry and Howard Dean, the two candidates for the Democratic nomination in 2004 who opted out of the public financing system. Their reason for wanting to do so was clear. Whoever won the nomination would face off against President Bush, who had raised $100 million for the 2000 race and eventually doubled that amount in the 2004 cycle. Moreover, Bush had no primary opponent in 2004, so he could focus all of his considerable campaign resources on positioning himself for the general election. If a Democratic nominee accepted public funding and the attendant spending limits, he would be placed at a severe disadvantage in the general election.

One of Kerry's attributes that made him an attractive candidate was his wealth. Kerry's wife was known to have a net worth in the hundreds of millions of dollars. By providing considerable personal funds to the campaign, Kerry could spend well beyond the $45 million allowed for candidates who accepted public funds. Contributing more than he could possibly receive in matching funds would allow him to position himself for the general election without harming his chances of winning the nomination. As Kerry's lawyers reviewed the matter, however, they noticed a major flaw in this argument. The vast majority of the family fortune belonged exclusively to his wife, Teresa Heinz Kerry, the widow of a Republican senator, John Heinz of Pennsylvania, and heir to the Heinz ketchup and condiments fortune. Given the way the Kerrys's finances were structured, most of their wealth clearly belonged to her and, therefore, could not be legally contributed to his campaign. The only way the Heinz money could be used was as an independent expenditure, but saying that the candidate's spouse was not coordinating with the candidate would be a difficult legal and political argument to make.

Kerry's advisers had to determine whether it made sense to reject public funding in the absence of a massive contribution by the candidate himself. The risk was that other campaigns, supplemented by matching funds, would be able to outspend Kerry during the nomination contest. In the fall of 2003, the Kerry campaign tentatively decided to accept the matching funds, but since the first round of federal matching funds would not be distributed until January, he had until the end of 2003 to make a final decision.

When the FEC publicly released the campaigns' third quarter 2003 financial disclosure reports, in October 2003, Howard Dean had surpassed Kerry as the top fundraiser in the race. As rumors had leaked out in the preceding month about Dean's fundraising success, he publicly speculated about not accepting public money. Given Dean's reliance on small contributions, refusing the matching funds would have been a larger sacrifice for his campaign than for any other. Moreover, Dean was not that far ahead of Kerry in fundraising and, given his pace, it would probably take the entire fourth quarter for him to make up for the lack of matching funds. While he clearly was raising money much faster than his rivals, he was not so far ahead that he could vastly outraise them without the matching funds.

In the end, the Dean campaign decided to forego public matching funds. The apparent deciding factor was the statewide spending limits. Dean gambled that he could win Iowa and New Hampshire by dramatically outspending his rivals in both states. This would provide him with the necessary momentum to win contests in the next round of primaries and make him the apparent nominee. By spending so much money in the first two states, however, he ran the risk of being outspent in the others. As it turned out, Dean placed third in Iowa and second in New Hampshire, leaving himself with no money, no momentum, and no hope of recovering.

Dean's decision forced the Kerry campaign to change course and reject public funding and spending limits. Kerry determined that he needed the flexibility to exceed the statewide limits in order to compete with Dean in Iowa and New Hampshire. He gave his campaign a quick injection of cash by borrowing $6 million against his share of the family fortune and poured it into the two opening contests. Once he beat Dean in both states, he had the best of both worlds—he had knocked off the only rival for the nomination who could compete with him financially and he did not have to worry about hitting the spending cap before the convention.

Are there other conditions under which it might make sense for a candidate to opt out of the public financing system? One problem that both Kerry and Dean faced was the flood of serious candidates in the race. For most of 2003, nine candidates whom the media considered serious sought the nomination. Six of them raised a substantial amount of money. There is only a limited number of people willing to contribute to presidential campaigns, thus the total pool of money available is finite. The more candidates there are in the race, the harder it is for any one of them to raise a large enough amount before the primaries to justify foregoing public funds. Similarly, in 2004 no candidate was able to separate himself from the pack enough to be deemed the clear front-runner for the nomination. If one had been able to do so it would have increased the flow of money into that campaign, since contributors like to go with a winner.

To sum up, there are three important factors that increase the likelihood that a candidate will choose to opt out of the public financing system.

1. The candidate is wealthy enough to finance his own campaign.
2. The number of candidates seeking the nomination is relatively small.
3. The candidate is the clear favorite for the nomination.

In short, candidates with a clear political advantage in winning the nomination can enhance that advantage by refusing matching funds and spending limits in order to prepare for the general election. A candidate that is back in the pack can do so only if he is independently wealthy.

Who Benefits?

The system for financing presidential nomination contests has four main ingredients. The core mechanism is a system involving spending limits at both the national and state levels supplemented by partial public financing. Candidates can, however, opt out of this system in favor of one with no spending limits and no public funding. Additionally, political parties can assist the nominee by spending money on "party-building activities" that are not coordinated with the campaign but help it nonetheless. Finally, other outside groups can make independent expenditures that aid their preferred candidate. Such spending by political parties and outside groups has been limited somewhat by the Bipartisan Campaign Reform Act of 2002, but it still plays an important role in the system. What type of candidate benefits from each of these four elements?

Public funds are available to match the first $250 of each contribution. Consequently, candidates with a broad base of contributors will receive more matching funds than those who do not have such a base. Candidates who begin the campaign with a large amount of support among party activists and other potential donors will benefit the most from this system. It is possible that another candidate could catch up by slowly building grassroots support over the course of the campaign, but one who already has a well-established national fundraising network can earn the matching funds much more easily.

Any candidate who can safely reject public financing in the primary is wise to do so because it enables him to exceed the spending limits. Every dollar spent to win the nomination also helps build positive name identification for the general election. Moreover, such candidates do not have to worry about running out of money in the months between the primaries and the convention because they can always raise more. However, campaigns are likely to take this path only if it does not significantly hurt their chances of winning the nomination. After all, if you don't get the party's nomination, you don't get to run in the general election. As discussed previously, the candidates who are in the best position to opt out of the FECA system are (1) independently wealthy candidates, (2) those who already have a large fundraising advantage over their competitors, and (3) those with few opponents. In other words, those who already have a significant fundraising edge can make that advantage overwhelming by ignoring the statewide and national spending limits; they can spend heavily in states with January and February primaries and caucuses to ensure that no upstart can gain momentum with an early upset victory.

Even though the national parties have the ability to spend money in support of their nominee, they are wary about being seen as interfering in the selection process. Consequently, they will not spend money in a way that benefits any particular candidate until after that candidate is the apparent winner. Thus, they do not directly affect the outcome at this stage of the process. However, the party does have an interest in having its nominee chosen quickly: it doesn't want the candidate to spend too much of his money fighting other same-party competitors for the nomination, and a quick victory in the nomination process allows the nominee to spend his own money on fighting the other party's nominee rather than relying heavily on party money. Consequently, once a single candidate seems to be breaking away from the pack, party leaders are tempted to anoint the winner and sideline the other candidates. To the extent that spending by the party has any effect on choosing the nominee, it benefits the candidate who gets off to a strong start in the early contests at the expense of underdog candidates seeking to gain momentum throughout the primary season.

Finally, outside groups can make independent expenditures in support of their preferred candidate. Once such a group has made its selection, it begins to help that candidate. However, if the group decides that there are multiple acceptable candidates, it may choose to wait until the race sorts itself out before spending any money. Again, this benefits the candidate who has a strong support base at the beginning of the process. Candidates trying to work their way out of the pack are much less likely to receive such support. In all respects then, the campaign finance system for presidential nomination contests favors the candidate who starts off with a robust support base and a network already in place to raise substantial money. In short, the mechanics of the system for choosing a presidential nominee favor the haves at the expense of the have-nots.

In the last two chapters, we have explored the mechanics of the delegate selection and fundraising processes. As in all competitive situations, the rules of the game affect the strategies of the players and the ultimate outcome—which candidate wins. What incentives does the system create for the various players in the process? What moves do the candidates make to win the game? What do party activists, campaign professionals, party chiefs, and interest group leaders do to achieve the selection of a candidate who best suits their interests? In the next chapter we will examine how these pieces come together in the selection of the candidate who will claim the mantle.

Notes

1. *Buckley v. Valeo*, 424 U.S. 1 (1976).

2. Data on contributions going back to 1996 can be found in a searchable database at the Federal Election Commission website, at www.fec.gov.

3. Campaign Finance Institute, *Participation, Competition, Engagement: Reviving and Improving Public Funding for Presidential Nomination Politics* (Washington, D.C.): Campaign Finance Institute, 2003), chapter 4.

4. Ibid.

5. Perot won 19 percent of the vote in the 1992 election. However, since he ran that race as an independent, no party benefited from his performance.

6. Buchanan eventually won the 1996 Reform Party nomination but gained less than 1 percent of the popular vote in the general election, making that party once again ineligible for public funding for 2004.

7. Diana Dwyre and Victoria A. Farrar-Myers, *Legislative Labyrinth: Congress and Campaign Finance Reform* (Washington, D.C.: Congressional Quarterly Press, 2001), pp. 18–19.

8. Ibid., pp. 21–28.

9. *McConnell v. FEC*, 124 S.Ct. 619 (2003).

10. John C. Green and Anthony Corrado, "The Impact of BCRA on Presidential Campaign Finance," in Michael J. Malbin, ed., *Life After Reform* (Lanham, Md.: Rowman & Littlefield, 2003).

4

Claiming the Mantle

To THIS POINT, WE have focused on the rules of the presidential nomination game. Now we turn our attention to the question that is foremost in the minds of everyone interested in politics: Who wins the nomination?

William Mayer presents a very clear answer to the question (see figure 4.1), demonstrating that the candidate who has raised the most money and is ahead in the polls on January 1 of the election year wins the nomination.[1] Of the ten contested presidential nomination races between 1980 and 2000, the candidate who reported raising the most money in the year before the election and the candidate who was ahead in the Gallup Poll at the beginning of the year won nine times.[2] Those are pretty good odds.

The 2004 Democratic race also defied Mayer's model: At the beginning of 2004, former Governor Howard Dean of Vermont was ahead in both the money chase and the polls, but by the time of the Iowa caucuses on January 19, his luster was beginning to fade. He came in a distant third in Iowa and the only primary he won was in his native Vermont. The nomination went instead to Senator John Kerry, the presumed favorite a year earlier, whose campaign had flagged in mid-2003 only to rise again in early 2004.

Even taking into account the 2004 results, Mayer's essential premise holds up—front-runners win. The primaries that blossomed under the 1970s reforms as a means of democratizing the process now rarely affect the outcome. Generally, the race is over before most voters have their say. This chapter begins by providing an institutional explanation for this phenomenon. How is it that the rules designed to democratize the process have instead fostered a system in which the casting of votes is essentially an afterthought?

The remainder of the chapter lays out the informal rules of the game. Who gets to be the front-runner? Why does one candidate claim

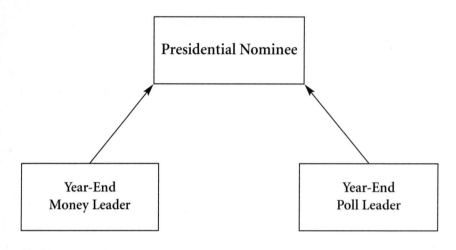

FIGURE 4.1   Mayer's Model of Presidential Nominations

the mantle while all the others fall short? If, as is usually the case, the candidate who leads in money and polls wins, the question still remains: How does a candidate get to the top in money and polls? And what else is required for a candidate to become the prohibitive frontrunner?

Institutions and Incentives

In chapters 2 and 3 we detailed the formal systems by which the delegates who select the nominee at the national convention are chosen and by which the candidates finance their campaigns. Some of the key factors were the following:

- A front-loaded primary schedule in which the Iowa and New Hampshire contests are followed quickly by blocks of states in the succeeding weeks
- A period of several months between the time that the nominee is known and the start of the general election campaign
- A campaign finance system based on spending limits (both national and statewide), contribution limits, and partial public financing

- The potential for candidates to opt out of the spending limits and matching funds
- The potential for parties and outside groups to spend money to affect the campaign

Every set of rules creates an incentive structure that guides the actions of the players. Let us examine those incentives for party leaders and candidates.

Incentives for Party Leaders

When we use the term "party leaders" we are really talking about several different types of people. One such group is the leadership of the national party—the members and officers of the Democratic and Republican national committees. In most cases their exclusive goal is to have a candidate that is best positioned to win the general election. A second group of leaders is the heads of the various ideological and policy constituencies that generally align themselves with the party; it is important to them that the nominee be ideologically acceptable. Elected officials are another group of party leaders. Like party officials, they want a nominee who is well positioned to win, but they have other goals as well. A presidential nominee that does not perform well within their own geographic region could harm party candidates further down the ballot and make it more difficult for the local party to recruit and retain members. Thus, like the heads of ideological groups, they may be more likely to take an active role in support of a presidential aspirant who will help their constituency.

Although the goals of the various leadership groups are somewhat different, the process provides incentives for all of them to act in the same way. The national party leaders want a nominee chosen quickly. National leaders' worst nightmare is a drawn-out nomination fight that drains significant resources from the nominee and splits the party into competing factions. Nor do they want their eventual candidate to hit the spending limit months before the convention. Although the national party committees have some resources they can use to promote the candidate, any such expenditures bite into money they have available to support senatorial, congressional, and gubernatorial candidates who will be on the ballot at the same time. Moreover, the banning of soft money by the Bipartisan Campaign Reform Act of 2002 has reduced the pool of funds available for activities that support the party's candidates for all offices. Thus, once a candidate looks as though he is likely to win the nomination, the national party committees have an incentive to rally around that candidate and push the others to the side.

The interests of ideological leaders create a similar rallying effect. As the campaign proceeds, some candidates will move into the top tier of potential winners while others lag behind. Suppose that one of those top-tier candidates is ideologically unacceptable to a particular wing of the party or to a group of policy constituencies. The leaders of those groups probably will rally behind a single acceptable candidate in order to block the unacceptable one. As in the case of national party leaders, this rallying effect serves to narrow the field of candidates and shorten the process.

Elected officials have to look out for the interests of both the local and the national parties. The former would lead them to rally behind a candidate who best serves their region; the latter leads them to rally behind (or at least not oppose) the front-runner once he emerges.

Even though the various types of party leaders have different goals, the rules of the nomination contest encourage them all to rally around the strongest candidates early, thereby shrinking the pack and ending the contest quickly.

Incentives for Candidates

As the major players in the game, candidates develop strategies to maximize the likelihood of their winning within the established rules. The mechanism that links rules and actions is different for candidates than for party leaders, but the result is similar. Candidates know that they must move to the head of the pack as early as possible in order to win the nomination. The nomination contest is really a race to claim the mantle—the first one to do so wins the prize.

Money is the lifeblood of a campaign. Without it, little is possible. Candidates operating within the formal structure know the maximum amount they can spend and are well advised to raise it as quickly as possible. Those who are considering opting out of the spending-limits system need to know as soon as possible how much they are likely to raise independently. Before a campaign can allocate resources efficiently, it must know how much is available. Consequently, if a candidate who plans to take public money is able to max out on matchable contributions early, he has no uncertainty about how much will eventually be available. Similarly, a candidate who plans to opt out of the public financing system has little uncertainty if he is on track to raise as much money as he has budgeted.

Suppose a candidate goes into the primary and caucus season without having raised all the money he is allowed to spend. The candidate then wins the Iowa caucuses and garners a great deal of publicity. This makes it much easier for the candidate to raise money. Nonetheless, having to raise money during the highly compressed primary season creates a number of problems. First, fundraising takes up some of the candidate's time that would be better spent communicating with voters through either personal visits or the mass media.

Second, uncertainty about the total amount of money that will be available adds a cloud of inefficiency to decisions as to how much money to allocate to each state contest. For example, the campaign cannot plan how much advertising to buy, and in which media markets, if it does not know how much money it has to spend.

Finally, the campaign will get less bang for the buck if it does not have money to spend in a state months before the primary is held. In a small-turnout primary election, the grassroots ground game is crucial. Yet get-out-the-vote activities like phone banks, canvassing, and election day mobilization take time to organize. A candidate who must simultaneously campaign and raise money for his nomination fight will be at a disadvantage in the ground war against an opponent who raised money early and has already set up a grassroots organization.

Clearly, the combination of the compressed schedule and fundraising restrictions places a great premium on pre-primary activities. Candidates who raise the money, create an organization, and build popular support before the first votes are cast have a virtually insurmountable advantage against those who do not. Underdogs may be able to compete with the front-runners in individual small contests such as Iowa and New Hampshire that reward retail politics, but they cannot do so when faced with campaigning in multiple large states that require massive media buys and extensive statewide organizations.

Candidates also know that party leaders are making their decisions on the basis of early performances. If you do not show promise, you are likely to be weeded out of the mix by elected officials and policy and constituency leaders. Once that happens, your ability to raise funds dries up and the race is over. To win, the candidate must move to the head of the pack early—he must claim the mantle.

Thus, the nomination process and the incentives it creates explain Mayer's findings. The candidate with the most money and the highest poll numbers at the beginning of the election year is almost guaranteed to win. Gaining the status of front-runner makes a candidate almost unbeatable. Knowing this, party leaders rally around the presumptive nominee to strengthen him for the general election. Yet, we still have not explored sufficiently how a candidate becomes the front-runner. How does the system decide which candidate is the front-runner before any votes are cast?

Mayer points to money and poll results as the predictors of who will win. However, we can already see that fundraising, poll results, and election results are so tightly connected that it is hard to tell which is the cause and which is the effect. Two factors make it hard to sort out the causal relationship. The first is the fact that in politics, perception often creates its own reality. A candidate who is perceived as the likely winner gains advantages over those who are not so perceived. Second, a full year before the general election, few voters are paying attention to presidential politics. Thus, their responses to poll questions are merely vague impressions based on limited information. Figure 4.2 illustrates the more complex relationship between the variables in Mayer's model showing the dynamics of the pre-primary phase.

Campaigns with a lot of money have more resources to use in their quest for the nomination—but how do they get more money in the first place? The perception that a candidate is likely to win also helps him raise money because high-dollar contributors would prefer to back the winner. They know that if they come on board early, they will have greater access to the administration to advance their own political agendas or to be appointed to an executive-branch position. If they back a loser, they have no such influence. The desire for influence, therefore, leads big contributors to donate to the candidate who is expected to win.

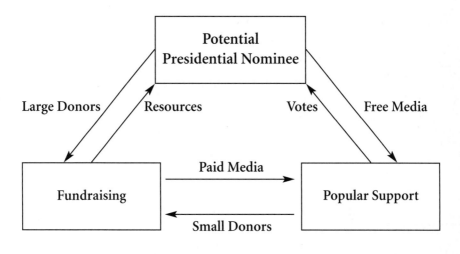

FIGURE 4.2   Dynamic Version of Mayer's Model of Presidential
Nominations

Poll results are one indicator of popular support, and the fact that few voters are paying attention to the race one year before a presidential election actually magnifies the influence of early polls. Thus, respondents have very little information upon which to base a decision; at best, they will know the names of a few of the candidates and have vague impressions of them from the media coverage. The potential nominee who can break through and establish name recognition as a candidate will have a great advantage. A candidate who is perceived as a likely nominee will get the most play on the television news, as will candidates who are already well known nationally. Because of the large number of uninformed respondents, poll results at this stage of the race are skewed toward those with high name recognition, either from their past accomplishments or from their being perceived as the front-runner. So there is a synergistic relationship between early poll results and the front-runner perception: early poll results are an indicator of who will win the nomination, and the perception of who will win the nomination affects the early poll results.

Fundraising and poll results are also bound tightly together. Candidates who have raised a lot of money early have already begun communicating their message to the voters. To the extent that they communicate effectively, the money they have spent on this boosts their poll numbers. Voters and activists who have heard the message and decided to support the candidate may make a contribution to the campaign. Thus, if rising poll numbers reflect the creation of informed grassroots support for the campaign, then the candidate should attract more small contributions. So, fundraising and poll results also have a circular effect on each other.

How to Claim the Mantle

By January of election year, we often can be fairly confident which candidate will win the nomination. At the very least, we can identify some candidates who have no serious chance of winning. Let us now examine the method by which candidates claim the mantle. Why are some able to raise lots of money while others are not? Why do some rise in the polls while others are stuck at the bottom? An examination of the thirteen contested presidential nomination contests since 1976 allows us to make certain generalizations that answer these questions.

Figure 4.3 shows the three main stages of any presidential nomination campaign. The first stage involves putting together the campaign *infrastructure*. As the first step, the candidate must begin raising money to finance the effort and putting together a campaign organization. The organization has a relatively small group of professionals responsible for the overall communications, fundraising, and outreach strategies. In addition to this professional core, the campaign must develop a very large, decentralized structure to coordinate activities and volunteers in every state.

Stage two is the *broadcast* stage of the campaign. It involves using institutions that reach large numbers of potential voters to gain wholesale support for the candidate. There are two steps within this stage. The first is to win the support of key constituency groups. If the leadership of important policy and ideological organizations backs your campaign—or at least deems you an acceptable choice—you have now accessed a large base of voters who rely on that group for political guidance. Even better, a policy group's endorsement may provide your campaign with a nationwide set of volunteers to supplement your own core organization. The second step is managing the media coverage of your campaign. The typical voter gets most of his or her information from the mass media. If the

The Infrastructure Stage

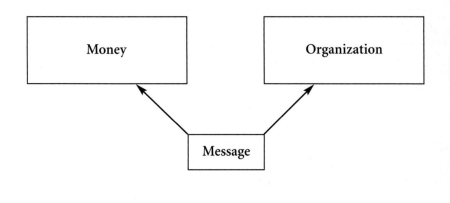

The Broadcast Stage

| Institutional Support | Media Management |

The Winnowing Stage

| Defeat Natural Rivals | Win Your Base, Be Competitive Elsewhere |

FIGURE 4.3   Requirements for Claiming the Mantle

press paints a positive image of your candidacy, low-information voters will gain a favorable impression of you and may well vote for you. If the media ignore your campaign, or criticize it, those same voters are unlikely to support you. Thus, media management is a vital ingredient in any presidential campaign.

Finally, stage three is the *winnowing* stage of the campaign. As some candidates succeed during the pre-primary campaign, others fall by the wayside. If no candidate has clearly claimed the mantle by the time of the first primaries and caucuses, the voters determine who will win the nomination. The candidate must demonstrate in the early primaries and caucuses that he is a winner and can run an effective general election campaign. A candidate must show quickly that not only does he have a strong natural base of support, but also that his candidacy is broadly acceptable. One way of doing this is to defeat the other candidates vying for the same base of support. Every campaign starts with an underlying constituency base or rationale for why it has the best candidate. If one candidate's base or rationale overlaps with another's, he must demonstrate his superiority over that candidate to avoid extensive competition for his market niche. Moreover, a candidate must win the primaries and caucuses he is expected to win and be competitive in those he is not expected to win. In an effort to keep from prolonging the process and bankrupting the eventual nominee, party leaders will rally around the first candidate to show such depth and breadth of support. Thus, the calendar becomes a key factor. To claim the mantle once the primaries have begun, a candidate needs the good fortune of demonstrating such support in states with early contests.

All three of these stages feed off of each other. The infrastructure stage begins first but can be affected by events that are part of the broadcast and winnowing stages as well. For example, the endorsement of an important interest group is likely to bring new contributors and volunteers into the campaign, enhancing the effectiveness of the campaign infrastructure. Good media coverage or winning an early primary can do the same thing. Similarly, later stages are strongly affected by the first stage. Constituency groups are unlikely to back a candidate who is not building a big enough war chest and organizational structure to run an effective campaign. Likewise, the media would cut back on its coverage of a candidate who is doing poorly in the first stage, reporting only that he is struggling. Success at each stage of the campaign enhances the success of all of the others.

Stage 1: Building a Campaign Infrastructure

At its core, an election campaign is an effort to persuade voters that a particular candidate is the best person for the job. No matter how skilled the candidate is, he cannot accomplish this task on the national level all by himself. He needs money to access the increasingly expensive tools of mass communication. He also needs other people to plan and implement his campaign and to help him deliver his message in a more personalized manner. In fact, the task of raising money and building an organization has become so enormous that the candidate needs to recruit people to help him create such a campaign infrastructure. Before he can convince voters to support him, the candidate needs the resources—the infrastructure—to craft a message that will attract activists to his cause. Without money and organization, a presidential candidate has no hope of winning the nomination.

Money

Many analysts call the pre-primary phase of the campaign "the money primary." While such a characterization is something of an oversimplification, the importance of money to a campaign cannot be overstated. Without money, a campaign cannot purchase the advertising needed to communicate to the immense pool of voters during the highly compressed primary schedule. And as we discussed earlier, it is much more difficult to spend money raised during the primary season in an efficient and effective manner. Thus, it is vital for the campaign to raise as much money as possible before the election year starts. In the best-case scenario, the campaign will raise every cent it plans to spend before the first vote is cast.

Raising money for a presidential nomination is a long and arduous process. Individual donors may not legally contribute more than $2,000 each to a candidate. If every contributor gave the maximum donation, the campaign would still need 22,500 contributors to reach the full $45 million dollar spending limit. Approaching potential donors individually, however, would be incredibly time consuming. The alternative approach is to send out direct mail solicitations to demographic groups who might have a natural affinity for the candidate. The problem with this approach is that a great deal of money in postage and labor must be spent in an effort to raise money. Because the response rate to such solicitations is tiny, this is also a highly inefficient process.

In recent presidential election cycles, as campaign spending has grown and the time to raise it has shrunk, two important innovations have facilitated the fundraising process. The first is known as *bundling*. Instead of finding thousands of donors, campaigns recruit fundraisers. Jeffrey Birnbaum describes this phenomenon in his book, *The Money Men*:

> Oddly, the most extraordinarily important, indispensable people in the fund-raising process are *not* the ones who have oodles of dollars to donate. That honor belongs to a group we should call the Solicitors: the politically active individuals who know lots of other people who are willing to donate a thousand dollars each to the candidates they back. . . . In the quirky world of campaign fund-raising, the most vital people aren't the check writers but the check *raisers*. [emphasis in original][3]

In his quest for the 2000 Republican nomination, George W. Bush recruited a group of such fundraisers. He established a club called the Pioneers for those people who raised at least $100,000 for the campaign. For 2004, with the rise in the individual contribution limit from $1,000 to $2,000, Bush added a new tier, called Rangers, for those raising at least $200,000. The Bush campaign website reported that as of August 11, 2004, it had recruited 333 Pioneers and 221 Rangers. By recruiting fundraisers instead of donors, campaigns are able to decentralize the process so that they minimize the time that the candidate and staff spend on solicitation from individual donors.

Another recent innovation is the use of the Internet for fundraising. Like direct mail, the Internet casts a very wide net to find small contributors, whose donations can be matched by public funds. Furthermore, there are no postage fees on the Internet and there is no delay for mail processing. John McCain, in 2000, was the first to utilize the Internet effectively as a fundraising tool. In 2004, Howard Dean made the

Internet the centerpiece of his fundraising operation as he sought the Democratic presidential nomination. By January 1, 2004, Dean had raised $41 million, mostly over the Internet. Whenever the campaign needed a fresh infusion of money, it would announce a fundraising drive on its website. Within a few days, hundreds of thousands of dollars would pour into the campaign coffers. The other candidates mimicked this strategy and leveraged every good primary showing into campaign cash. Once John Kerry clinched the 2004 nomination, his Internet fundraising skyrocketed. People who had contributed to his rivals and those who were waiting for a winner to emerge flooded his website with contributions. The campaign estimated that it collected $56 million in online contributions during the first half of 2004.[4]

Dean's fundraising success was a perfect example of the importance of money in presidential politics. At the beginning of the race, Dean was not considered a serious contender. The media portrayed him as a gadfly preaching the true Democratic religion who was destined for an early exit from the campaign. However, when the Federal Election Commission released its second-quarter fundraising reports in July 2003, Dean was in a nip-and-tuck battle with Senator John Kerry for the leadership in money raised. Instantly, Dean vaulted into the top tier of potential nominees and had his picture on the cover of *Time* and *Newsweek* simultaneously in August. By contrast, Senator Joseph Lieberman of Connecticut, the party's 2000 nominee for vice president, showed weak fundraising on the second-quarter reports. The media shifted the tone of its coverage of Lieberman from that of a leading candidate to that of a voice in the wilderness pleading for moderation. A campaign must raise a lot of money early to avoid being viewed as a lost cause.

Organization

The first step in building a campaign organization is recruiting a strong team of experienced consultants to oversee the campaign activities. These top jobs include the campaign manager, the finance director, and the media consultant. Every political consultant dreams of one day playing a major role in a winning presidential campaign. Consequently, the top-tier consultants choose the candidates they will work with carefully, seeking out a candidate who best matches their own personal ideology and has a chance to win. Snagging one of these consultants signals to party activists and the media that the candidate is putting together a team that could potentially go all the way.

Building an organization for a presidential campaign capable of competing all across the country is an extraordinarily labor-intensive process. After Iowa and New Hampshire, the campaign's central staff can no longer focus its attention narrowly on a single contest at a time; the campaign must have a highly decentralized operation. It takes an army of volunteers to hand out literature, operate phone banks, talk to their neighbors, write letters to the editor, hold candidate house parties, and undertake other grassroots activities. And they *must* be volunteers. A campaign that paid people to perform these duties would use up a massive amount of money that otherwise could have been used for broadcast advertising that communicates with voters by the thousands. As with fundraising, the key to accomplishing this task is to recruit the recruiters. If a candidate wins the support of office holders and other party leaders, they can, in turn, create an organization.

Anyone who has ever won elective office has had to build her own organization and, if she expects to win again, that organization must be current and functional. This office holder can play a crucial role in another politician's campaign: she can deliver her organization in the service of his campaign, and the campaign that wins her support will inherit her volunteers. This goes for high-level office holders, local party officials, and political leaders of all sorts. Thus, the shortcut to building a massive decentralized organization is to win over those who already have organizations handy.

One way to win the support of office holders and local party leaders is to do favors for as many of them as possible. In the two years prior to the presidential election cycle, people considering a presidential run raise money and campaign for candidates from all over the country, particularly those in important primary and caucus states. The potential presidential candidates finance these operations by establishing a fund known as a leadership PAC. Like other political action committees, leadership PACs gather funds in increments of up to $2,000 and can give up to $5,000 to a candidate for office. Presidential aspirants also use this money to finance political travel so that they can headline fundraising events for candidates across the country.[5] These activities make local officials and party organizations more amenable once the presidential wannabe announces his candidacy and asks for their support. By helping out other politicians years before the presidential contest begins, candidates groom potential supporters who will help them build a formidable organization in key states.

Such efforts suffice in most states, but Iowa and New Hampshire are different. Residents of these two states are proud of their "first-in-the-nation" status and take their responsibility as candidate winnowers seriously. They expect to meet the candidates personally to size them up. Since Iowa and New Hampshire are both relatively small states, it is possible for candidates over time to meet a substantial percentage of the voters. In these two vital states, organizations are built one person at a time with no middlemen involved.

This presents an opportunity for underdog candidates. They can camp out in Iowa and New Hampshire for weeks at a time to build a grassroots organization and develop personal support. Jimmy Carter was one of the first candidates to adopt this strategy. After making numerous trips to the state, some as early as 1972, this little-known former governor of Georgia won the 1976 Iowa caucuses, gaining national acclaim that he rode all the way to the White House.[6] Since then, Iowa and New Hampshire have been perceived as the salvation for the underdog who cannot afford to build a multistate organization.

Message

The common theme running through the quest for money and organization is a campaign's ability to attract activists as supporters. They need to get fundraisers with long lists of potential donors to gather in the money needed to finance a national campaign. They also need elected officials and party activists to volunteer their time to build a grassroots organization that will span the country. How do they attract these activists to the campaign? They present a compelling message that convinces the activists to come on board.

It is often hard to know at the beginning of a presidential cycle what message will be effective in attracting support. Each candidate has to present a coherent rationale as to why he or she should be the nominee. In the end, one will turn out to have made the most compelling case, but it is often not obvious which one it will be. The cases that candidates make for themselves fall into seven general categories.

I can win.   Political activists want to win elections. Thus, a coherent argument as to why the candidate has the best chance of winning both the nomination and the general election can be compelling. Victory means that the party agenda can be advanced, and early supporters have an advantage in gaining the ear of the administration once in office. It also opens up a number of political positions that will likely go to those who supported the campaign during the primaries. In making this case, candidates have to convince potential supporters of how they can win both the nomination and the general election.

Thematic message.   One way of winning a national election is to craft a message that will appeal not only to one's own party but also to independent voters and persuadable backers of the opposition. A message is much broader than a series of issue positions. It is a coherent and comprehensive formulation of one's approach to governing. It is, in short, what President George H. W. Bush dismissed as "the vision thing."

Two recent examples of successful presidential campaign themes illustrate what we mean by "message." George W. Bush (who clearly understood the concept of campaign message better than his father) ran in 2000 on a program of "compassionate conservatism." This formulation can be summarized as a federal government that is limited in scope but focuses on providing people in need with the tools to become self-sufficient. This statement of governing approach attracted voters who would normally be wary of conservative policies but could feel comfortable with Bush. Similarly, in the 1992 election campaign, Bill Clinton spoke frequently of creating a "new covenant" between government and the people whereby the government would provide services for the people but citizens would be required to take greater responsibility for their own lives and for their communities. This bridging of themes from the right and left (coupled with the use of overtly religious language in the moniker to attract southern and rural voters) expanded Clinton's appeal and helped him win the White House.

Issue positioning.   During some election seasons, there is a single galvanizing issue that dominates the campaign—one issue so important or so controversial that it dominates the political debate. In such an environment, an aspiring nominee may try to convince activists that he would be the best candidate to exploit the perceived issue vulnerability of the other party. During 2003 and 2004, the Iraq War dominated the political debate and spurred passionate opposition within the Democratic Party. Most of the Democratic nominees flocked to the issue, trying to convince the party that their own position on the issue gave the party the best opportunity to attack the incumbent president. Some did so by demonstrating their passionate opposition to the war right from the start. Others took the position that they had supported giving the President the authority to go to war in order to enhance his bargaining position, but they opposed the President's tactics and indicated that they would have built an international coalition before using force.

Résumé. Presidential nominees are not just baskets of issue positions or promises that they can win. They are individuals with unique perspectives and abilities derived from their personal histories. Candidates may try to convince party activists that their own life story provides them with some measure of credibility on important political issues that the others lack. The 2004 election took place under the cloud of the War on Terrorism launched after the September 11, 2001, attacks on the World Trade Center and the Pentagon. Voters might have been reluctant to choose a Democrat for the position of commander in chief during a time of war given the party's perceived dovishness in the wake of Vietnam. Senator John Kerry, a Vietnam veteran who had been awarded the Silver Star for his combat service, argued that his war experience would make him the best nominee. He would have credibility as a potential commander in chief that the other candidates lacked. In this way, Kerry tried to convince the party that his own life story would make him the best nominee.

Campaign skills. The candidate has to convince potential supporters that he has the basic skills needed to run an effective campaign. Activists will generally make this assessment on the basis of previous campaigns run by the candidate, usually for lower office. For example, if he has had trouble raising enough money in past races, party activists will worry that he will be unable to mount an effective presidential campaign. Similarly, candidates whose previous races suffered from ineffective central leadership, poor strategy, inability to connect with voters, or poor debate performances may have trouble drawing supporters who are looking for a winner. However, most candidates know their weaknesses and will work to assuage such concerns. For example, some activists were wary of backing the Gephardt campaign in the 2004 cycle because he had not raised enough money in his 1988 bid for the White House. To compensate, Gephardt put a lot of effort (with only mixed success) into early fundraising in order to ease the concerns of potential backers.

Party positioning.   All of the above arguments can work only if the party activists think the general election will be close. If they think that their party will win in a romp, or that they have no chance of winning in November, other factors will dominate their choice as to whom they will support.

If the general election outcome will not be affected by the party's choice of a candidate, then the party is likely to concentrate on its own internal politics in making a selection. They can use their choice of a presidential nominee to position the party for the long term. They ask themselves which factions they wish to lead the party, or how they can position the party to achieve long-term political dominance. These considerations were important factors in the 2004 Democratic presidential nominating contest. Having been shut out of control of the White House, the House of Representatives, and the Senate after the 2002 congressional elections, Democrats were split over the best strategy to regain power. Some argued that the party needed to move more to the center to attract swing voters. Others argued that the party needed to oppose Republican policies more strenuously. Still others thought that the key lay in crafting a set of alternative solutions to present to the voters. This struggle dominated the 2004 nomination process as each of the candidates laid out his case as to which direction the party should go and why he was the best leader to take it there.

Inevitability.   Finally, there is one argument that a potential nominee might be able to make that trumps all others. In some presidential cycles, one candidate stands out above the others long before the process begins. The moment one election is over, everyone knows who is the front-runner for the nomination four years later. This candidate may be the incumbent president or vice president, or a powerful figure widely recognized as the voice of the party. Such a candidate need only say to the fundraisers and party activists: "You know I am going to be the nominee. The train is leaving the station. Either get on board now or get left behind." This is a powerful message. People will reject it only if their opposition to the candidate is intense because they know that failing to support the inevitable nominee early will leave them out in the cold when it comes to any influence they might have once that candidate becomes President.

Thus, activists are only likely to abandon the "inevitable" favorite if a large number of others are willing to do likewise. For this reason, sitting presidents and vice presidents seeking the nomination have faced serious challenges only if they have alienated the base of the party. The only groups that have the passion and the numbers to put a scare into a front-runner are core constituencies. For example, Jimmy Carter was challenged from the left in 1980 once the left wing of the party perceived him as too timid on health-care reform, and George H. W. Bush was challenged from the right in 1992 after he broke his "no new taxes" pledge. If the heir apparent has not alienated the base, no challenger will be able to raise the money or build the organization necessary for a credible race, so the heir apparent can claim the mantle virtually unopposed.

Stage 2: Broadcasting the Message

Running for president is not like running for local office; it is not possible to shake hands with every constituent and ask for his or her vote. The Iowa caucuses and the New Hampshire primary demand this sort of personal contact, but following these events the candidates must move rapidly to persuade millions of voters in a short period of time. To make this transition from retail to wholesale politics—to connect with so many people—presidential campaigns must tap into preexisting organizational and communications networks.

The political system is full of organized groups, each of which has its own constituents and the means to contact them. Gaining the support of such groups provides a candidate with instant credibility among a sizable number of voters. Broadcast media give candidates the means to present their message to millions of voters simultaneously. In order to win the nomination, a candidate needs to use these ready-made tools to broadcast his message widely and advance his campaign.

Broadcasting via Constituency Groups

It is feasible to win voters a handful at a time in Iowa and New Hampshire. Once the candidate has to compete in multiple states simultaneously, however, he must communicate to voters thousands at a time. One way to accomplish this is to win the support of the leaders of various constituencies and ideological factions that make up the base of the party. These groups have institutional structures and long lists of supporters that they can mobilize for or against a candidate. By winning over these leaders, the campaign inherits a strong foundation of money, organization, and votes.

The ultimate accomplishment is to win the endorsement of major party factions. If a key constituency anoints a candidate as its choice for the presidency, it can throw its resources behind that campaign. It can use its membership rolls to find and mobilize a cadre of volunteers throughout the country. It can also use its own money for independent expenditures that indirectly aid the campaign. Finally, once a group supports a candidate, it can convince its members to vote for that person. Since these groups have a national reach, they can be a big help in creating a grassroots organization in a large number of states simultaneously.

The best example of a candidate trying to accomplish this task in 2004 was Dick Gephardt's courtship of the AFL-CIO. In order to win the endorsement of the entire labor movement, Gephardt needed the support of individual unions that represented at least two thirds of the AFL-CIO's overall membership. Gephardt spent months courting these unions while the other campaigns tried equally hard to block him from getting labor's full support. In the end, Gephardt did not receive the endorsement of the AFL-CIO, but he did get the backing of over twenty separate unions.[7] In November 2003, these unions pooled their resources to run ads supporting his candidacy in the crucial state of Iowa. This augmented Gephardt's own campaign spending beyond the official statewide limits established by the FEC.[8]

No candidate in a competitive race will win the endorsement of every constituency group; still, candidates must avoid being deemed unacceptable by any major group. Suppose you are a candidate who has alienated a key constituency in the party and you begin surging to the head of the pack. That constituency will then throw its full support behind the strongest candidate it finds acceptable in an effort to keep you from winning. This gives a boost to your opponent, who will now inherit the abundant financial and organizational resources of that group. If you had managed to stay in the good graces of that constituency, your opponent would not have benefited from your progress. The best example of this in 2004 was the effort by nearly every campaign to woo the antiwar movement. This new constituency was loosely organized through the Internet but incredibly energized. Even the candidates who had voted in Congress to grant President Bush the authority to attack Iraq adjusted their positions to make them acceptable to this movement.

Managing the Media

Key constituency groups can mobilize large numbers of potential voters and volunteers, but candidates must take into account the power of the media, a permanent institution with a broader reach than any one constituent group. The media are the primary source of political information for most citizens. Thus, a candidate who manages to get favorable press coverage can amplify his message exponentially without having to spend a dime.

As the primary season approaches, candidates can purchase unfettered access to the media by buying advertising time. Television and radio are flooded with campaign commercials, inundating voters with messages that tout the views, accomplishments, and personal qualities of the candidate while deriding those of his opponents. However, airtime for television commercials has to be purchased and candidates are limited in how much they are able to raise and spend. Thus, it is not possible for campaigns to have consistent unfiltered access to the voters over the airwaves for months on end prior to a state's nomination contest.

During the long pre-primary phase, therefore, candidates must rely on the news and entertainment media to provide information to the vast number of people who will eventually choose the nominee. Such coverage has the virtue of being free. However, by depending on news organizations, the campaign loses control over both the amount of coverage and the content. The media decide how much airtime to give each campaign at any given time and what to say about the candidate. Since the media are the major source of political information to voters, it is vital for a campaign to manage the media skillfully so that voters get a lot of exposure to the candidate and so that the messages they receive are positive ones.

Throughout the campaign, the media will pay attention to certain predictable milestones and other expected and unexpected events of various kinds. These the media are guaranteed to cover. Candidates try to perform as well as possible for the events they know are coming so that the media will tell voters about how successful their campaign is. At other times, the media use opinion polls to find concrete evidence of how well the candidates are doing at attracting the support of voters. The rest of the time, campaigns engage in a more subtle game of convincing the various news outlets that they are performing well, that they have the potential to win the nomination, and that they are worthy of the prize. There are a number of ways for candidates to capture positive media attention.

Quarterly fundraising reports.   The Federal Election Campaign Act requires all candidates to submit quarterly reports to the Federal Election Commission detailing the source and quantity of all contributions and expenditures during the reporting period. This is the sort of concrete data that the media pounce on, and they are guaranteed to report and analyze the data and what it suggests about the viability of each campaign.

Knowing this, campaigns make a concerted effort to raise as much as they possibly can in the final weeks of the reporting period. They push their contributors to send the money in immediately so that it will show up in the current report. That way, the media are more likely to report that their campaign is making good progress at raising money and, hopefully, is doing well compared to the other candidates.

Such news stories have several real effects on a campaign. First, they signal to potential donors and organizers which candidates have a serious chance to win the nomination. This may encourage them to sign on to the campaign in the future. To borrow an expression from a Washington-based fundraising organization, "Early money is like yeast, it makes the dough rise."[9] Second, such stories signal to voters that the campaign is going well. At this stage of the game, few voters pay very much attention to the race. However, if they hear from the media that a campaign is raising a lot of money, they are likely to get a positive impression that they will carry with them until the next big news event of the campaign. Finally, it gives the media a reason to continue covering your campaign. Once the members of the media think your campaign is hopeless, it is very difficult to get anything through their filter and onto the airwaves.

A good example of how these reports can affect media coverage occurred after the June 30, 2003, FEC reports were filed. The three leading money raisers were John Kerry, Howard Dean, and Senator John Edwards of North Carolina. Kerry, as the initial presumptive frontrunner, continued receiving good press coverage because he had performed as expected. Governor Dean had not been getting much coverage because he was considered a minor candidate. Now, however, because he raised as much money as the big boys, the media vaulted him into its top tier of candidates and began covering his campaign accordingly. Edwards's money came mostly from a narrow base of big-money contributors. Since media analysts were uncertain whether he could broaden his base enough to keep up the pace, they took a wait-and-see attitude toward his campaign. By contrast, Senator Joe Lieberman, who had been Al Gore's running mate in 2000 and consequently an automatic top-tier candidate in 2004, raised little money in the first half of the year. The press reported that his campaign was faltering, and he never recovered.

Polls.   The press loves to cover the horse race. One easy way to report hard information about the state of the nomination contest is to conduct a public opinion poll to find out voter preferences among the candidates. When such polls are taken months before the first votes are cast, they provide very little useful information. Since voters are not yet following the campaign, they have no way of assessing which candidate they prefer. Consequently, these polls reflect little more than name recognition. In effect, they are measures of how effective the campaigns have been at managing the media.

Such polls can, however, provide useful information if their results defy expectations. Candidates who have achieved national visibility, perhaps from previous runs for president or vice president, are expected to poll well. If they do not, it is a sign that the voters know them and don't like them. It is very difficult for candidates to overcome such negative first impressions. Alternatively, if a relatively unknown candidate keeps moving up in the polls, it is a sign that a number of voters have noticed him and like what they see.

As the first primaries and caucuses approach, public opinion polls become more meaningful. More voters tune into the race and begin gathering the information they need to formulate an opinion of the candidates. This is particularly true in the states holding early primaries and caucuses. The media escalate the number of polls they conduct of voter preferences nationwide and of those in the early-primary states. The statewide polls in particular provide some indication of whether or not the candidates are winning over voters.

Straw polls. In an effort to gain attention from the candidates, some state parties hold a straw poll in the year before the primaries and caucuses. The Iowa Republican Party has traditionally held one at the State Fair, and both Florida parties have done so at their state conventions. To cast a straw-poll ballot, participants generally have to pay a fee or register well in advance to attend the convention. They may also have to travel a long distance to attend the event at the specified time and place.

These straw polls are like mini-primaries. Though they have no direct impact on the selection of delegates, they do serve a purpose. Campaigns view them as an opportunity to demonstrate their candidate's popularity and their own organizational abilities, and candidates give speeches to the faithful party activists to win their votes. The trick to winning a straw poll is getting more of your supporters to attend than another campaign. A straw poll can only be won by a determined grassroots organization that contacts party stalwarts one by one. The media are sure to cover these events because they are real votes cast by real voters. They are also indicators of each candidate's ability to build an organization and mount a successful election campaign. Many underdogs have spent a lot of money trying to do well in straw polls in order to get a heavy dose of positive media coverage to jump-start their campaigns.

On the other hand, straw polls have also proved to be the last nail in the coffin of struggling campaigns. In August 1999, most of the Republican candidates for president mounted extensive efforts to win the

Iowa straw poll. After poor showings in the straw poll, Congressman John Kasich of Ohio and Lamar Alexander, a former governor of Tennessee, already trailing badly in the money race, withdrew their presidential candidacies months before the first votes were cast. In 2004, the Democratic National Committee successfully opposed the holding of straw polls, fearing that campaigning for them would unnecessarily drain precious resources from the candidates' coffers.[10]

Debates and interviews.   Debates have become one of the staples of presidential campaigns. Ever since the Kennedy-Nixon debates of 1960, all presidential candidates have felt obliged to debate their opponents. The trend has also spread to the nomination contests. Candidates receive hundreds of invitations to participate in debates, with more and more taking place every cycle. Many of these are covered by either national or local media. In that respect, we can consider them big events that candidates need to use to their own advantage.

However, debates have reached the point of diminishing marginal returns. There are now so many debates that they do not seem particularly special. For the 2004 cycle, the Democratic National Committee sanctioned only a limited number of these proposed debates so that candidates did not feel obligated to waste precious time participating in all of them. The potential of a candidate's debate performance to help or harm his nomination prospects varies depending on the timing of the debate and the number of participants.

Media coverage of a debate provides candidates with a forum to speak directly to voters without having their remarks filtered by the press. Unfortunately, most voters do not pay attention to the campaign months before the first primary, so not many will actually receive the full, unabridged version of the candidate's message. This limits the ability of the candidate to win over voters through a debate performance. The problem is exacerbated when there are many candidates in the field and each one gets to have the floor for only a small chunk of time in the course of the debate, so that no coherent message is possible. It is hard to convince people of anything when you are limited to a few one-minute responses and thirty-second rebuttals for the whole evening.

In crowded early debates, the best a candidate can hope for is to get off a pithy one-liner that will make the evening news and the morning shows the next day. Few voters watch the full debate, so they will only see what makes it through the media filter. Consequently, these debates seem more like a contest to see who can come up with the best sound bite than an effort to inform voters. However, if a candidate makes some big mistake, that will also show up on the evening news much to his dismay. Early debates, therefore, have lost much of their potency in the nomination process.

Later in the campaign season, however, debates can serve their desired function and have a far greater impact than in the early stages. With fewer candidates left in the race, each one has more time to discuss his issue positions and demonstrate his personal qualities to the voters. Moreover, the viewership for such debates is much higher because more voters have begun to pay attention to the race. These debates provide a campaign with the ability to speak directly to voters without the media filter. A good performance will be highlighted for days in the media, as will a candidate's most embarrassing moment. These are the sorts of events in which candidates must think on their feet and show themselves at their best.

Another media format, the Sunday morning chat shows, provides voters and the press with a clearer look at the candidates. Five different networks have programs on Sunday morning in which top journalists interview Washington figures. These shows are watched by all of political Washington and play a major role in shaping establishment opinion in the capital city. In the run-up to the primaries, the networks invite all of the candidates to appear on these programs.[11]

Because of the extended format of these programs, candidates have the time to make a firm impression on voters and on the Washington political community. A strong performance can earn a candidate a great deal of respect because he will have survived a probing interview with plenty of opportunity for follow-up questions. Conversely, a weak performance seriously harms the candidate's credibility among the movers and shakers because they view him as "not ready for prime time." Such candidates will have a difficult time building institutional support for their campaigns until they repair the damage.

Beating the rap. Most national political correspondents have covered many presidential campaigns over the years. During that time, they have seen for themselves the qualities needed in a successful campaign, and they also know the strengths and weaknesses of the big-time players in Washington. Consequently, longtime journalists have a ready-made reference frame for analyzing the major candidates. They know in what areas he will be expected to excel as well as the flaws he will need to overcome in order to win the nomination. The first hurdle that lesser-known candidates have to clear is demonstrating that they are serious candidates so the media will take notice. They can accomplish this by raising a lot of money or building support in the polls.

The next hurdle is that journalists and media professionals soon recognize both the underlying strengths of the candidate and also spot the weaknesses. Candidates need to show the press that they are overcoming their weaknesses. In short, they must beat the media rap. If they do not, the press will pounce on any mistake or underperformance in that particular area as emblematic of a flawed campaign. Avoiding such problems shows the press that the candidate is stronger than they anticipated, and the coverage will reflect this newfound respect.

Examples of candidates with a rap sheet abounded in the 2004 nomination contest. Senator John Kerry was seen as an aloof figure who had a hard time connecting with the voters. Senator John Edwards's only political experience was four years in the Senate, so the press wondered whether he had a firm grasp of the issues. Reporters wondered whether Howard Dean's angry populist rhetoric would keep him from looking "presidential" to the voters.

Kerry was the only one of these candidates to beat the media rap. He got warm receptions in Iowa, showing that he could connect with voters one-on-one. After that, his media coverage got much more positive. Edwards's disastrous performance on *Meet the Press* in May 2003 crystallized the media's belief the he was a political lightweight. It took Edwards months to reestablish his presidential credentials. And who can forget Howard Dean's Iowa concession speech? Trying to energize his youthful supporters, Dean adopted the gravelly baritone of a professional wrestler and concluded with a scream that Walt Whitman might have called a "barbaric yawp." The networks replayed it thousands of times in the following week on their news broadcasts, morning programs, and late-night comedy shows, making Dean the butt of a giant national joke. He never beat that rap.

Taking a punch.   At some point in the presidential nomination contest, each candidate with a serious prospect of winning the nomination will be subjected to a media feeding frenzy of bad publicity. The galvanizing story can take many forms. Often it involves some activity in the candidate's past that he finds difficult to explain. Or perhaps the candidate says something really stupid on the campaign trail that becomes the talk of the press corps. Alternatively, the candidate may perform unexpectedly poorly in a primary, raising questions about his viability as a candidate.

Stories like this have the potential to sink a campaign if the candidate does not find some way to get out of the tailspin. One method is to change the subject. If the candidate can find a positive story big enough to get the media's attention, they may drop the bad story in favor of the good. Alternatively, the story may die quickly if no new details emerge. That is why candidates are best served by laying out all of the information they can about whatever "scandal" is causing the feeding frenzy. Otherwise, the slow drip of information will keep the story alive and overshadow the candidate's message. Finally, the best way to overcome an unexpected primary loss is to start winning again. If a candidate is well organized in later states, he can win them despite some early stumbles. But if he has not already built a firewall, the downward momentum can sink his campaign.

The expectations game.   Once we go beyond fundraising totals and primary victories, the criteria used by the media to assess campaigns become very subjective. What separates a good performance from a bad one? The measuring stick is expectations. Did the candidate do better or worse than expected?

There are two sources for the level of expectations surrounding any campaign event. One is the media, which uses its own analytic judgment to predict how well a candidate should do. The more important source, however, is the campaign itself. In public interviews and background conversations, the media often ask the candidates and their senior campaign staff about their strategy and expectations. Campaigns are well advised to lowball their estimates as much as they possibly can. The lower they can push the expectations bar, the more likely they are to exceed it.

An excellent example of good and bad expectations management occurred in the 2004 Democratic nomination battle. The Kerry campaign, which had been lagging in the polls for months, decided to campaign heavily in Iowa, but Kerry constantly downplayed his expectations there. The party line in the Kerry campaign was that he had started late in Iowa and it was far from his New England base, so they would be happy to come in as low as third. When Kerry unexpectedly won the Iowa caucuses, he got an enormous media bounce that catapulted him to a big win in New Hampshire and victories in five of the seven states that held their contests the following week.

By contrast, the Dean campaign made it very clear that they were aiming for an early knockout. They spent millions of dollars in both Iowa and New Hampshire, boldly predicting that they would win the primary or caucus in all fifty states. When Dean came in a distant third in Iowa, the air came out of his campaign. His poll numbers plummeted everywhere and he had no firewall set up in later states to help him bounce back. Instead of winning every contest in the nation, Dean lost all but Vermont.

Competition for Media's Attention.   In some presidential nomination cycles, a candidate may find himself competing for media attention against more than just his rivals within his own party—the other party's presidential nomination contest can impact the outcome of one's own race. If both parties have contested nominations, the available airtime is spread thinner, and if one party has an exciting race going on, candidates in the other party will have a hard time getting any attention whatsoever.

The most recent example of this phenomenon occurred in 2000. After John McCain upset George W. Bush in the New Hampshire primary, the Republican contest was the hot story that garnered the most media attention. Meanwhile, Bill Bradley was trying to mount a comeback in his race with Al Gore for the Democratic nomination after losing to Gore in Iowa and New Hampshire, but with journalists busy reporting on the more exciting Republican race, Bradley was able to get only limited press attention. He had no way of changing the image voters had established in their mind of his being beaten by Gore in the two early contests. With voters' perceptions of the race locked in and no new Bradley message getting out, Gore swept the remaining primaries and caucuses.

Stage 3: Winnowing the Pack

As a presidential campaign progresses, some candidates demonstrate that they are potential winners and others show that they are not. The losers are weeded out and the potential winners receive all of the money and attention. The pace of this winnowing varies from race to race, but history does point to one determining event. After the New Hampshire primary, very few candidates will still be considered viable, usually no more than three. It is vital, therefore, for a candidate to remain in that top tier as it gets smaller and smaller.

Defeating Natural Rivals

As the field is culled to the final few, there is only room for one candidate who fills a particular niche in the race. From the start, each candidate will have enunciated a rationale for his campaign regarding his vision, issue positioning, geographic base, experience, and so forth. To make it into the top tier, a candidate must clearly rise above the others who have a similar rationale. If he falls behind or runs even with those candidates, there will not be room enough for him among the final few. He must, therefore, defeat his natural rivals, those whose message or constituency is closest to his own.

The most direct route to defeating your natural rivals is if none enter the race. If no other candidates have a rationale that overlaps yours, you do not have to spend the time and effort needed to defeat them. Thus, a candidate's strategy can be greatly affected by which other candidates enter the race. If natural rivals enter, you must focus your early attention on beating them. If not, you can work to shore up your own un-contested base, while making inroads with those outside your natural constituency. In 2004, Dick Gephardt was the candidate who benefited most in this regard. Senate Democratic Leader Tom Daschle of South Dakota had been widely expected to seek the presidential nomination. Gephardt and Daschle were both experienced party leaders from the Midwest with strong ties to rural America. As they used to say in the old westerns, "This town ain't big enough for the both of them." Neither one would be able to focus on beating the rest of the field until he had knocked off the other. Gephardt was the happiest man in Washington when Daschle announced in January 2003 that he would not enter the race. Gephardt had a niche all to himself while all of the other candidates had natural rivals to beat. (Having a niche to himself from the beginning did not ultimately help Gephardt. He dropped out of the race on January 20 after finishing a distant fourth in the Iowa caucuses.)

A candidate does not have to wait for the primary season to begin before he defeats his natural rivals. There are plenty of pre-primary indicators that a candidate is surpassing one or more other candidates. For example, if one candidate far outpaces his natural rivals in fundraising, he may demonstrate his dominance over them, causing their campaigns to wither on the vine. Polling results and debate performances can accomplish the same thing. When Howard Dean first entered the nomination contest for 2004, he was viewed as an outside-the-Beltway candidate futilely railing against the system. However, Carol Moseley Braun of Illinois, Dennis Kucinich of Ohio, and Al Sharpton of New York were viewed in the same light. There was only room for one candidate in the "outsider" niche, so the first contest was between these four to see who would make the cut. Dean massively out-fundraised the other three in the early reporting periods and established himself as *the* outsider candidate. Having won that honor, he was able to turn his attention to expanding his appeal to the rest of the party.

If no candidate clearly defeats his natural rivals in the pre-primary phase, he must do so at the ballot box. Early in the primary season, such a candidate must soundly beat his rivals in a primary or caucus that reflects both candidates' base. For example, when General Wesley Clark entered the 2004 contest, the rationale for his campaign overlapped those of two others already in the race. He and Kerry both argued that their military experience would give them the credibility to compete with President Bush on foreign policy. The major difference between the two was that Clark was from the South (Arkansas) and Kerry was from New England. The geographic angle to Clark's campaign placed him in competition with North Carolina's John Edwards, who was arguing that only he could win over southern voters in the general election. As it turned out, Kerry outpaced Clark in both northern and southern primaries, thereby claiming the "war hero" slot in the race. Neither Clark nor Edwards, however, clearly outperformed the other in the early primaries so neither one was able to establish himself instantly as *the* alternative to Kerry. Eventually, Edwards pulled ahead of Clark, but he had lost valuable time.

The Primary Phase

As these examples indicate, if no single candidate has claimed the mantle before the Iowa caucuses, then the voters themselves get to choose the party's nominee. Since no candidate has yet claimed the mantle, none has gained such an overwhelming advantage that his eventual nomination is assured. Despite the apparent positive value of voters getting to select their candidate, it is not in fact in the best interest of the party for this competition to continue for very long because every dollar spent on choosing a nominee is a dollar that cannot be spent to defeat the other party's candidate. Thus, the candidate whose primary and caucus performances first stand out from the pack will be the one whom the party rallies around and anoints.

It is crucial, therefore, for the candidates to demonstrate in the primaries that they have the ability to run a competitive general election campaign. This means that they must have a strong base of support plus the ability to win votes from a broad cross-section of the country. To borrow a sports metaphor, the candidates must show that they can win the home games handily and be very competitive in the road games. Since the party wants to choose its nominee as quickly as possible, each candidate needs to find some early contests that will allow him to demonstrate both of these traits.

Thus, the calendar becomes an important factor when nominations are still up in the air during the primary season. A candidate examining the schedule of early contests will look for some states that are a part of his natural base and some others in which he can run near the top. If, instead, he sees a bunch of early states in which he cannot run a competitive race, he has no hope of winning the nomination.

Iowa and New Hampshire have been the first two contests in every election since the reforms of the 1970s and so they are the states that provide the first opportunity for candidates to demonstrate their national electability.[12] Rural and midwestern candidates must win the Iowa caucuses or else they will be viewed as paper tigers unable to hold their own base. The same is true for New England candidates with respect to New Hampshire. Other candidates must run near the head of the pack in one of these states to show that they are competitive outside of their natural base. The winnowing process is so rapid by this stage of the game that conventional wisdom suggests that there are, at most, only three tickets out of New Hampshire. Some campaigns have tried to bypass these two states and jump-start their campaign later, but invariably they have failed because the media attention given to the candidates who did well in Iowa and New Hampshire drowns out everyone else.

From that point on, the compressed calendar provides ample opportunity for the final few to show their electability. Within weeks, each candidate will likely face contests in states that are part of his base, states in another candidate's base, and states that are neutral territory. The successful candidate will be the one who wins his base states, wins the neutral states, and finishes a strong second (or preferably first) in another candidate's base states. As soon as possible, the party will rally behind the candidate who has best demonstrated this capability, and for all intents and purposes, the nominee is selected.

Summary

Often, one candidate for the presidential nomination is so dominant in the pre-primary phase that he claims the mantle before any votes are cast. There are two stages in the pre-primary phase, each of which has multiple elements, and a campaign must excel in all of them if he is to put himself in such a position. The first stage involves raising money and building an organization. Because of the cumbersome campaign finance rules and the decentralized nature of successful organizations, it takes a great deal of time and effort to perform them properly. Consequently, it is necessary for the candidate to get help from outside sources.

In order to raise millions of dollars in intervals of $2,000 or less, candidates recruit fundraisers who can approach their own contacts for contributions. This bundling procedure puts many people to work in support of the candidate. Alternatively, the candidate can now focus on soliciting funds via the Internet. This is a low-cost technique but it typically brings in only small contributions. Building a nationwide organization begins with the upper echelon of the campaign staff, but must also spread out widely across the country. Again, the only way to accomplish this in a short period of time is to recruit some recruiters. Once a campaign finds someone to organize each state, that person then recruits organizers at the local level. Eventually, a nationwide organization springs up out of the grassroots.

Every campaign tries to recruit from the pool of fundraisers, campaign professionals, and grassroots organizers. The candidate who will be most successful is the one who can provide a compelling rationale for his campaign. Identifying the right message is vital because these potential volunteers and staff are looking for a winner. The candidate must convince them that he is the one they should support. As a result, the process of raising money and building an organization helps the candidate hone the message he will use in the campaign.

Having convinced potential supporters one-on-one to support the campaign, the candidate next needs to broadcast his message to a wide spectrum of voters by gathering institutional support and managing the media. Local elected officials and interest group leaders have their own networks of supporters. Once the candidate gets them on board, they will announce to their organizations that they are supporting the candidate in an effort to gain their own members' support as well. Gaining institutional support provides a megaphone to spread the message much more broadly, and more cheaply, than the candidate ever could.

The biggest megaphone of all is the media. The campaign needs to find ways to get the media to talk about the candidate in a positive light. Voters, who are paying little attention to the campaign at this time, hear good things about the candidate and gain a positive impression of him. In particular, the candidates must perform better than expected in measurable aspects of the campaign such as fundraising and polls. They must also convince the pundits that their own relative weaknesses are not serious enough to prevent them from getting the nomination.

If no single candidate dominates the pre-primary phase, the voters pick the winner. In addition to excelling in the pre-primary activities, candidates must survive the winnowing process by beating their natural rivals. As the field narrows, there will only be a few spots available, so there is not enough room for two similar candidates. Moreover, the candidate must demonstrate that he can win contests among his base voters and perform well in other states as well. As soon as one candidate clearly demonstrates that he can do both of these better than the others, the party will rally behind him to end the process as quickly as possible. They hope to avoid having the candidate spend all of his money winning the nomination and be left struggling during the long period between the early primaries and the convention. For this reason, even when the voters get a say in choosing the nominee, only those in a few early states really have a voice. Sometimes, a small percentage of the voters matter; other times none of them do.

Notes

1. William G. Mayer, "Forecasting Presidential Nominations, or, My Model Worked Just Fine, Thank You," *PS: Political Science and Politics* 36, no. 2 (2003): 153–57.

2. The first exception was the 1980 Republican nomination, in which John Connally raised the most money but Ronald Reagan won the prize; the second exception was the 1988 Democratic nomination, in which Gary Hart led the polls in January but Michael Dukakis won the race.

3. Jeffrey H. Birnbaum, *The Money Men: The Real Story of Fund-raising's Influence on Political Power in America* (New York: Crown, 2000), p. 50.

4. Glen Justice, "Clicking into the Kerry Coffers for a One-Day Online Record," *New York Times*, July 2, 2004.

5. Presidential candidates also have used their leadership PAC funds to circumvent the spending limits. Before announcing their candidacies, they would use the PAC money for "political travel" that, in effect, was part of their formative presidential campaign efforts. In December 2003, the Federal Election Commission ruled that this practice violated the spending limits and began to scrutinize such expenditures more carefully.

6. Actually, Carter came in second, behind "uncommitted," but he beat all of the other candidates in the race.

7. Howard Dean won the endorsement of two very large unions representing service-sector workers and government employees. Most of the other AFL-CIO member unions made no endorsement before the primaries began.

8. Union support proved insufficient to boost Gephardt's sagging campaign in Iowa. He placed fourth in the January 19 Iowa caucuses and ended his quest for the presidency the next day.

9. The phrase was popularized by EMILY's List (note the acronym), which raises money for pro-choice Democratic women candidates for federal office.

10. The only straw poll during the 2004 election cycle was held in the District of Columbia six days before the Iowa caucuses. The purpose of the event was to draw attention

to the District's lack of voting representation in the Congress. Only four of the nine major presidential candidates participated in the straw poll and it had no impact on the race.

11. In the 2004 cycle, these appearances were unofficially dubbed the "Russert primary," after Tim Russert, the tenacious host of NBC's *Meet the Press*.

12. The Republican Party of Michigan in 1988 and Louisiana in 1996 developed drawn-out, convoluted delegate selection processes that began before Iowa and New Hampshire. In those cases, some of the leading candidates competed in contests to choose the people who would later choose the delegates to the national convention. Michigan and the District of Columbia tried similar plans for 2004 but were blocked by the Democratic National Committee. The DNC threatened to withhold recognition of the two convention delegations, so both backed down.

PART II

PLAYING THE GAME

5

The Seven Dwarfs

In 2004, a large field of Democrats battled through the pre-primary period until a winner emerged, several weeks after the New Hampshire primary. In 2000, George W. Bush waited to see which Republican candidate would emerge from a crowded field to be his principal rival and then crushed him. The 2000 Democratic contest shaped up early as a battle between two Democratic heavyweights. Though these three contests played out differently, they ended quickly.

These nomination contests are prototypes of the three possible scenarios that can arise from the pre-primary phase of the campaign. The next three chapters will examine each in turn and show how they operate. In two of the scenarios the outcome is predetermined: the front-runner will win no matter what. In the third scenario the winner is less predictable, but we know that the game will be over in short order.

This typology of the structure of nomination contests is similar to one crafted by Larry Bartels, a Princeton University professor of political science. In his book, *Presidential Primaries and the Dynamics of Public Choice*, Bartels distinguishes among three types of primary campaigns: those with no major candidates, those with one major candidate, and those with two major candidates.[1] Our three categories differ from Bartels's in that we classify the campaigns according to how many candidates emerge from the pre-primary phase in a dominant position. Thus, our categories permit a candidate who begins the process as a virtual unknown to claim the mantle, while a well-known candidate may fall back in the pack.

In this chapter, we begin the discussion of the three types of presidential nomination games with those contests—typified by the 2004 Democratic race—in which no candidate emerges from the pre-primary phase in a clearly dominant position, based on the factors discussed in chapter 4. Using a phrase that was popularized in 1988 as a description of the seven Democratic candidates, we call this the "Seven Dwarfs" scenario.

In chapter 6, we examine races in which a number of lesser candidates compete against a single heir apparent or, as with the Republicans in 2000, against a single candidate who claims the mantle during the pre-primary phase. We call this scenario "Snow White and the Seven Dwarfs." Finally, in chapter 7, we examine competitions between two major figures who are leaders of different wings of the party. We call this "Clash of the Titans."

The "Seven Dwarfs" Scenario

This type of race is the most unpredictable because we cannot be certain until after the primaries have begun which one of several potential winners will emerge triumphant. Under this scenario, the field narrows throughout the pre-primary phase of the campaign until there are only a few left standing with a realistic chance at victory. As the pre-primary phase progresses, the field separates into potential winners and sure losers. Thus, we see candidates fall by the wayside long before they formally drop out of the race, leaving it to others to compete for the title. Once the voters begin to cast their ballots, a winner quickly emerges.

Adding to the scenario's unpredictability are several subjective elements in the process of claiming the mantle. One such element is the rationale of the various campaigns. None of the Seven Dwarfs impresses party leaders and activists enough so that they can agree he is the best choice. It may be that leaders and activists are split over what kind of candidate would be best for the upcoming election or for the long-term health of the party. In this case, different party factions may support different candidates, canceling each other out so that there is no clear favorite. In addition, individual party leaders and activists may be genuinely uncertain about what their party needs. Such hesitation makes it difficult for them to view any candidate as ideal, so they are unwilling to commit enthusiastically to any contender. Alternatively, there may be a unity about what the party needs, but none of the candidates particularly fits the bill. Thus, individual party leaders and activists may reach different conclusions as to which candidate would be the best nominee for that particular election. Uncertainty regarding the fundamental question of what qualities to look for in a candidate makes it more difficult for us to forecast which one will eventually prevail.

Another reason why we cannot predict in advance which of the Seven Dwarfs will prevail is that the standard of success is fluid. In general, success at every stage of the race is defined by whether the candidate has exceeded expectations. If he does so, he will gain a leg up in the race; if not, it could be fatal. The level of expectations for a candidate is set both by the campaign and by the media. Candidates typically try to set the bar very low for their performance in fundraising, opinion polls, debates, and straw polls, so that it will be easy to exceed expectations. The media, however, use their own experience to handicap the various demonstrations of campaign support. This intermingling of campaign spin and media analysis cannot be predicted in advance, but we see its impact as some candidates falter while others soar.

Finally, a few hundred votes can make all the difference in the world as to which candidates survive the winnowing process. The first and most important contests are in Iowa and New Hampshire, two relatively small states. In a multicandidate field, a small number of votes can mark the difference between a second- and a fourth-place finish. The former can launch a candidate into the top tier while the latter can cause the press to view that candidate as a loser.

During the pre-primary phase, the Seven Dwarfs game is one of survival, not victory. In the year before the primaries, each candidate faces a series of public indicators of his campaign's strength. To remain a viable candidate, each must demonstrate that his campaign is progressing to a potentially successful conclusion. If the media and the pundits conclude that a candidate is failing these tests, his campaign is doomed. Once the experts conclude that he has no chance of winning, his fundraising dries up, his ability to build an organization deteriorates, and the prophecy becomes self-fulfilling.

One important set of events in this process is the quarterly fundraising reports mandated by the Federal Election Commission (FEC). Each campaign is required to disclose how much money it has raised and spent during the three-month periods ending March 31, June 30, September 30, and December 31. These reports are due by the fifteenth day of the following month and the media have a field day with the numbers. The FEC's data make it easy for the media to compare the relative strength of each candidate in gathering the most important fuel needed to run a campaign: money. Candidates who have fallen far behind their rivals in fundraising had better have a good explanation and a plan to do better next quarter. Otherwise, they risk falling out of the top tier of candidates and having their entire campaign effort sputter and stall like a car that has run out of gas.

National public opinion polls are another means of gauging the success of individual campaigns. Throughout the pre-primary season, media organizations, polling companies, and universities take periodic polls of those eligible to choose the party's nominee to determine which candidate they favor. The earliest of these polls are tests of name recognition rather than popularity because few voters are paying attention to the race and so the best-known candidates always lead these early polls. Consequently, the goal for the other candidates is to show steady progress. As the months pass, they need rising poll numbers to demonstrate their support is growing. Candidates with polling numbers that appear stuck at low levels risk being viewed as nonviable.

National polls are not the only ones that matter. Local media outlets and polling firms specializing in statewide surveys regularly measure candidate support in early primary and caucus states. Election analysts map out the key states for each candidate on the basis of their natural geographic and philosophical ties, and of the public statements the individual campaigns make about their strategy. Thus, it is crucial for campaigns to demonstrate growing support in the states where they expect to win.

In most presidential election cycles, a few state parties hold straw polls during the summer before the primaries. These have become another means by which campaigns can demonstrate public support for their candidacies. Two states that have regularly held such events are Iowa, in conjunction with its state fair, and Florida, at the state party convention. Unlike opinion polls, straw polls require participants to actually show up to cast their votes. Thus, they are as much an indicator of the strength of a candidate's organization as they are of his public support. These events draw heavy media attention, so campaigns will devote a lot of resources to performing well in them. For this reason, the Democratic National Committee actively (and successfully) discouraged states from holding straw polls in 2003, deeming them a waste of candidate resources. In the past, however, they have been major events that shaped the nomination contest. For example, after the

Iowa straw poll in the summer of 1999, several major candidates dropped out of the race for the 2000 Republican nomination.

Fundraising reports, opinion polls, and straw polls act as objective measures of the more subtle indicators of campaign success during the pre-primary phase. They provide unspinnable evidence of the candidates' ability to raise money, build an organization, attract institutional support, and court voters. Thus, they are the events that tend to divide the field into the top tier and the also-rans in the year prior to the primaries. Once they have winnowed the field to the final few, the early primaries and caucuses pick the winner. To continue the Seven Dwarfs metaphor, one dwarf will do well in the early primaries and is transformed into Snow White once the party rallies behind him.

Two other characters often make an appearance in the Seven Dwarfs scenario. The fact that the party has begun to rally around a single candidate after the early primaries does not mean that all of the other candidates will immediately drop out. Sometimes, a second candidate survives the winnowing process but trails Snow White badly in the amount of money and number of delegates accumulated. This candidate (let's call him Doc, the leader of the Dwarfs) stays in the race pursuing Snow White as long as he can. He will probably even win a few primaries, or at least come close, as voters begin to have second thoughts about Snow White. However, Doc does not have the resources to catch Snow White and he is bound to fail.

Often, a third candidate will keep competing all the way to the convention despite the fact that he has no chance of victory. He seeks not to win but to send a message. Like a latter-day Howard Beale from the 1976 film *Network*, he takes to the airwaves with a simple message: "I'm as mad as hell and I'm not going to take this anymore!" Let's call him Grumpy. Grumpy can survive without money or an organization because he can mobilize the true believers using local radio and television. By convention time, he is Snow White's only remaining challenger.

The Democratic contests of 1976, 1988, 1992, and 2004 were examples of the "Seven Dwarfs" scenario. Because they span the entire era after the reforms of the early seventies, these contests demonstrate how the process has evolved so that the length of the nomination race has shortened over the years.

The Republican Party has never seen a "Seven Dwarfs" scenario in choosing its nominee. From 1976 through 1996, the Republicans always had a clear heir at the end of one election cycle who was ready to claim the mantle four years later. Although there was no obvious heir to the throne after the 1996 election, George W. Bush claimed that title during the pre-primary phase. Because of this history, some analysts refer to the Republicans as the party of primogeniture, in which all the power passes immediately to the next in line for the highest office.

Democrats, 1976:
Jimmy Carter Writes the Dwarf Handbook

The 1976 presidential campaign marked a transitional year for the presidential nomination process. The rules for allocating delegates had been in place for a full cycle, but states were still sorting out how best to choose their convention delegates. Similarly, candidates were still trying to determine the best strategy to win the nomination. Everyone had watched George McGovern create a grassroots movement of anti-war activists that swept him to the 1972 nomination. Yet after McGovern was trounced in the general election, neither party leaders nor candidates were confident that this was the best way to choose a presidential nominee.

The changes in campaign finance regulations were still in limbo as the 1976 campaign got under way. The Federal Election Campaign Act amendments of 1974 were scheduled to take effect in January 1975. Thus, candidates for the 1976 nomination were not bound by the $1,000-per-person contribution limits on money raised before that date. As the cycle proceeded, problems arose. Congress did not appropriate the federal matching funds on time, so candidates who were counting on that income stream to finance their campaigns were left high and dry in the spring of 1976.

After the Democrats' general-election debacle of 1972, the early front-runner for the nomination in 1976 was Senator Edward Kennedy of Massachusetts. Kennedy was clearly the leader of the liberal wing of the Democratic Party. Moreover, he likely would be a strong candidate in the general election, owing to the public's intense emotional connection with his family in the wake of the assassination of his two brothers.

Since everyone expected him to run in 1976, no candidates who shared Kennedy's support base were preparing campaigns in 1973 and 1974.

Only three other candidates were laying the groundwork to challenge Kennedy for the nomination. One was Senator Henry (Scoop) Jackson of Washington. Jackson was very much a New Deal labor Democrat on economic issues. However, he remained a hawk on foreign policy and a traditionalist on social issues. These positions meant that he was out of step with the post-Vietnam Democratic activists, who considered him a party moderate.[2]

The other well-known candidate planning to run for the 1976 nomination was Governor George Wallace of Alabama. Wallace had sought the Democratic nomination for president several times in the past, running on a segregationist platform. In 1968, he bolted the party and ran for president on the American Independent Party ticket, winning 13.5 percent of the popular vote and 46 electoral votes from southern states. In 1972, he returned to seek the Democratic nomination, but his quest ended abruptly when he was shot and paralyzed in an assassination attempt while campaigning in Laurel, Maryland. Although Wallace had separated himself somewhat from his segregationist past in his 1974 gubernatorial campaign, he was still anathema to most of the Democratic Party. In addition, his lack of mobility and weakened health had decimated his stem-winding oratory and one-on-one campaign skills, which had won him so many votes in the past.[3]

Finally, there was Jimmy Carter, a one-term governor of Georgia. Unaware of Jackson's impending campaign, Carter saw himself as the perfect alternative to Kennedy and Wallace. He believed that the party faithful would realize that Kennedy would be too liberal to win the general election. Carter believed he was positioned perfectly for the nomination—a southerner who would not be tarred as either a liberal northerner or a segregationist. He was part of the new breed of southern politicians who won votes from both whites and African Americans.[4]

On September 23, 1974, Ted Kennedy shocked the political world by announcing that he would not seek the nomination. Suddenly, the post-Watergate liberal wing of the party found itself without a standard bearer. In the following year, eight candidates jumped into the race to fill Kennedy's shoes. The most notable of these were Congressman Mo Udall of Arizona, Senator Fred Harris of Oklahoma, Senator Birch Bayh of Indiana, and Sargent Shriver of Maryland, who was Kennedy's brother-in-law and had run for vice president on McGovern's ticket. Governor Jerry Brown of California and Idaho Senator Frank Church signaled that they might eventually jump into the race. Former Vice President (and 1968 presidential nominee) Hubert Humphrey of Minnesota also hinted that he was willing to accept the nomination if the party turned to him. All of these candidates, however, got off to a very late start and none was Kennedy's logical heir as the liberal standard bearer.

Jimmy Carter appears to have been the only candidate in the race who learned from McGovern's success in winning the nomination. Although Carter did not have at his disposal an enormous grassroots movement like McGovern's, he saw that McGovern's strategy was perfectly suited to the presidential nomination process. In a series of campaign memos drafted in 1972, Carter's aide, Hamilton Jordan, laid out a strategy that had Carter spend three years traveling the country to introduce himself to party leaders and local activists in states with early nomination contests. He believed that Carter could do well in Iowa and other states that had caucuses in January, and win the New Hampshire primary in February. In that way, he would build up enough momentum to carry the larger industrial states that held their primaries later in 1976. Carter facilitated this strategy by becoming the Democratic National Committee's campaign chair for the 1974 congressional election cycle. In that capacity he traveled to sixty-two different congressional districts and met local Democratic officials and activists from all over the country.[5]

No other candidate adopted this sort of strategy. The eight liberals, as natural rivals, first had to fight each other before they could turn their attention to Carter, Jackson, and Wallace. Thus, they focused on winning over constituency leaders and primary voters in liberal strongholds. Scoop Jackson, who had taken second place in numerous 1972 primaries, felt that he had to start off as a winner to shake the stigma of being an also-ran. His natural base was among union households and Jewish voters. Thus, he focused on the industrial states and Florida to the exclusion of all else. He wanted to "win the big ones."[6] Wallace's appeal was limited almost exclusively to the South. He targeted primaries in southern states and also contests in certain northern states; one of these was Massachusetts, where busing was a hot issue. He financed his campaign through contributions from his previous supporters, raising $6.9 million via direct mail.[7]

Carter spent 1975 traveling the country giving speeches and conducting town hall meetings. Thus, he built a national organization from the ground up with scores of volunteers in all of the early primary and caucus states. He demonstrated the early strength of his organization by winning a "practice Iowa caucus" in the summer of 1975, bringing national media attention to his campaign.[8] As an example of the difference between Carter and everybody else, Bayh, Udall, Harris, and Jackson spent December 1975 trying to gain the unified endorsements of state party leaders at conventions in New York and Massachusetts. But not one of the four succeeded because none of them received the supermajority from the convention delegates in either state that was a prerequisite to gaining the endorsements. Thus, these four sank a lot of money into a failed effort to defeat their natural rivals. This weakened their ability to take on Carter, who was already amassing a nationwide organization.[9]

By Labor Day of 1975, Carter had moved to Iowa to campaign virtually full-time there. In January 1976, some of the other candidates began to campaign there heavily as well, but they lacked a network of volunteers like the one Carter had been building for months. On January 20, Carter outdistanced his rivals by winning 28 percent of the Iowa vote, followed by Bayh with 13 percent, Harris with 10 percent, and all the others in single digits (37 percent of Iowa caucus participants opted for uncommitted delegates). In a string of caucuses over the next few weeks, Carter placed second behind Wallace in Mississippi, dealt a major blow to the Harris campaign by tying him in his home state of Oklahoma, and won in Maine. On February 24, Carter won the New Hampshire primary with 30 percent of the vote. Udall, who had targeted New Hampshire for an early victory, took second with 24 percent, followed by Bayh at 16 percent and Harris at 11 percent. Carter's strategy was working brilliantly as this early burst of momentum won him convention delegates from all over the country, provided positive national media coverage, and increased his fundraising.

Months would pass before Udall could prevail over the other liberal candidates and turn his attention to defeating Carter. Even then, Harris

kept hanging on, siphoning critical votes away from him. Consequently, Udall did not come in first in any primary or caucus, and his
campaign stalled as a result. When Carter defeated him on April 6 in
the traditionally liberal Wisconsin, Udall's campaign was over. Because
of his ill health, Wallace was unable to rekindle the spark of his previous campaigns, and his loss to Carter in Florida on March 9 ended his
hopes of winning the nomination.

Despite Udall's defeat, the liberal wing of the party was not yet ready
to rally behind Carter. Two new candidates, California Governor Jerry
Brown and Senator Frank Church of Idaho jumped into the contest in
April. Brown won the contests in California and three other states
while Church won a handful of western and prairie states. However,
Carter performed well everywhere, methodically building his delegate
total. Because of their late start, neither Brown nor Church could run
the nationwide campaign necessary to win the nomination outright.

Scoop Jackson did not contest a state during the first two months of
1976. His first big effort came in Massachusetts on March 2, where he
won with 23 percent of the vote. Having skipped the early caucuses,
Jackson needed a burst of victories to gain momentum, so he decided to
contest Florida the next week. He came in third. By limiting the number
of states in which he would compete, Jackson lost media coverage and
momentum, and his fundraising stalled. To attract media attention, he
boldly predicted victories in New York and Pennsylvania. He won New
York on April 6 but placed a distant second to Carter three weeks later
in Pennsylvania. Out of money and without the expected infusion of
matching funds, Jackson brought his candidacy to a close.

By the end of the primary season on June 8, Carter was far ahead of
all of the candidates in the delegate chase, but was still short of the
1,505 he needed for a first-ballot victory at the convention, to be held
in New York. The party was faced with a choice of unifying behind
Carter or having a fractious brokered convention. Most of the defeated
candidates decided to endorse Carter and the party rallied behind him.
Carter had written the playbook that would be used by every underdog
candidate in later years: Campaign heavily in the early states. Use a
"better-than-expected" performance there to gain momentum and
money. Leverage that into support in the larger states that come later in
the process. Among his other accomplishments, Jimmy Carter was the

author of the handbook on how a Dwarf can transform himself into Snow White and claim the mantle.

Democrats, 1988: Snow White Falls and Can't Get Up

The early front-runner for the 1988 Democratic presidential nomination was Gary Hart, a former senator from Colorado. In 1984, Hart had used an unexpectedly strong second-place finish in Iowa to catapult himself to victory in New Hampshire. This performance made him the principal rival to former Vice President Walter Mondale of Minnesota, the party's anointed heir. Although Mondale went on to beat him decisively in 1984, Hart continued his quest for the presidency, making himself the clear favorite for 1988.

Late in 1986, rumors of Hart's marital infidelity swirled around his campaign. In response to a question about this, Hart challenged reporters to follow him around, claiming that they would get bored very quickly. One reporter from the *Miami Herald* clandestinely took Hart up on his suggestion—and was not bored. In December 1986, the reporter discovered Hart spending the weekend in his Washington, D.C., townhouse with a young model named Donna Rice. Pictures surfaced and Hart exited the race. Nobody wrested the mantle from Gary Hart's grasp—he threw it away.

Despite the collapse of the Hart campaign, Democrats remained optimistic about regaining the White House in the 1988 election. President Reagan was ineligible for reelection, and his final years in office had been tainted by scandal. Democrats believed they had an excellent opportunity to defeat Reagan's vice president, George H. W. Bush, but with Hart's demise they were left without a nationally known candidate. Instead, they had to choose from a group of potential nominees, each of whom had a strong geographic base. Among them were Governor Michael Dukakis of Massachusetts, representing the Northeast; Congressman Dick Gephardt of Missouri and Senator Paul Simon of Illinois, representing the Midwest; and Senator Al Gore of Tennessee, who ran as a southern moderate. The Reverend Jesse Jackson, who had run in 1984, had a strong base of support in African American and urban communities. The candidate best able to expand beyond his natural base would claim the mantle.

The 1988 election marked the advent of Super Tuesday—a large bloc of states holding primaries on the same day. Southern states had moved their primaries to March 8 in an effort to gain leverage in the nomination process. A number of others also jumped into the mix, creating a de facto national primary three weeks after New Hampshire, in which sixteen states, eight of them in the South, held primaries and four others held caucuses.

By 1988, Jimmy Carter's strategy of 1976 had become the model for all non-front-runner presidential campaigns. Thus, each candidate studied the calendar to figure out where he could score an early victory that would propel him ahead of the pack to the nomination. Michael Dukakis planned to do well in Iowa to demonstrate his national appeal, win New Hampshire (where he was the overwhelming favorite as the governor of a neighboring state), then pick up a lot of delegates on Super Tuesday from the northern states and from pockets of support in the South. At that point, he would be the front-runner and would coast to victory.[10] To run such a national campaign, he would have to raise a lot of money early. In the first quarter of his candidacy, Dukakis raised $4.2 million—far more than any of his rivals—and collected $1 million a month after that.[11]

Paul Simon and Dick Gephardt, as natural rivals from the Midwest, had very similar strategies. Each needed to win Iowa to demonstrate strength in his base. That would vault them to a strong showing in New Hampshire. They would then return to the rural Midwest for caucuses in South Dakota and Minnesota and ride that momentum to a large delegate pickup on Super Tuesday. Later in March, they would wrap up the nomination with victories in Illinois and Michigan.[12] The two candidates shared the same game plan—but one of them would first have to beat the other soundly for the strategy to work.

Al Gore, a hawkish southern candidate who was running on a more moderate platform than the rest of the field, saw himself as the natural beneficiary of Super Tuesday. His plan was to win the South and the position himself as the electable alternative to whichever liberal survived the early contests. However, he saw little hope of doing well in dovish Iowa or in Dukakis's backyard in New Hampshire. Fearing that a series of early poor performances would cripple his campaign before

Super Tuesday, Gore skipped Iowa in order to launch his campaign in the South.[13]

Lastly, Jesse Jackson had developed a strong base of support in urban and African-American communities during his 1984 run for the nomination. Jackson's goal this time was to expand his base to create a "Rainbow Coalition" of the dispossessed. This would give him much broader appeal, allowing him to accumulate far more delegates than he had in 1984.

Gephardt, Simon, and Dukakis led the pack in Iowa in the months prior to the caucuses. Gephardt took the early lead on the basis of his having spent forty-one days in Iowa before his formal campaign announcement in February 1987.[14] He faded as a result of some weak debate performances but surged at the end after a large advertising blitz. Simon rose in the Iowa polls every time another liberal candidate dropped out of the race, but he faded after Hart got back in the race in December 1987.[15] Hart's comeback effort never gained any momentum. Having tossed away the mantle, he was nothing but a Dwarf with no money and no organization. Meanwhile, Dukakis rose steadily in the polls as he introduced himself more and more to Iowans. In the end, Gephardt squeaked out a narrow victory with 31 percent of the vote followed by Simon with 27 percent and Dukakis at 22 percent. For Dukakis, coming in a close third behind two midwestern candidates was the solid showing he needed. Gephardt, however, failed to deliver a knockout blow to Simon. New Hampshire provided a similar outcome: Dukakis won (as expected), garnering 36 percent of the vote, followed by Gephardt at 20 percent and Simon at 17 percent. Dukakis got the result he needed; Gephardt and Simon did not.

With the Minnesota and South Dakota caucuses, Gephardt and Simon had another opportunity to score a victory before Super Tuesday. Because neither candidate had pulled ahead of the other, neither was able to turn victories into campaign contributions. Both were low on funds and each focused on only one of these two caucus states. Gephardt won South Dakota, but came in fourth behind Dukakis, Jackson, and Simon in Minnesota.

As Super Tuesday arrived with so many viable candidates still in the field, none of them needed to receive a majority of the votes in order to win a lot of delegates. Dukakis focused on the northern states and his pockets of support in the South: liberal enclaves, southern Florida's Jewish community (Dukakis's wife is Jewish), and Hispanic communities (Dukakis speaks Spanish). Jackson mobilized the large southern African American vote. Gephardt, who had poured the bulk of his money and resources into Iowa, had little capacity to build new support. Gore campaigned hard among white southerners, but was competing with Gephardt for their votes. Simon did not contest Super Tuesday, hoping instead to jump-start his campaign in his home-state primary in Illinois. Across the Super Tuesday states, Dukakis captured 26 percent of the vote and 356 delegates, leading the pack in nine states. Gore also won 26 percent of the vote but only six states and 318 delegates. Jackson won four states while Gephardt won only his native Missouri.

After Super Tuesday, Dukakis was the only candidate who was running a national campaign, piling up delegates in every state. Gephardt, Gore, and Simon each searched for targets of opportunity, but their campaigns never regained traction. Jackson took on the role of "Grumpy," doing well in a number of states with large urban populations—even winning Michigan. However, he had no chance of winning the nomination. He hoped instead to garner enough convention delegates to have an influence on the platform debates. With his strong showings in Iowa, New Hampshire, and southern Super Tuesday states, Dukakis locked down his base and demonstrated nationwide appeal. Dukakis claimed the mantle.

Democrats, 1992: The Comeback Dwarf

The 1992 Democratic presidential nomination contest got started later than usual. The Gulf War in early 1991 and its aftermath put potential candidates on hold as they paused to reconsider their strategies. Moreover, President Bush's soaring popularity immediately after the war made many candidates wonder if the prize was worth having. Bush appeared unbeatable.

Announcement season came in the second half of 1991, as the men touted by the media as potential candidates came forward to reveal their plans. This time, there were as many candidates announcing that they would not run as there were declaring their candidacy. Three also-rans from 1988 (Dick Gephardt, Al Gore, and Jesse Jackson) announced that they would not seek the nomination this time around. Senator Jay Rockefeller of West Virginia, who seemed to be preparing for a presidential race, decided not to do so. And New York Governor Mario Cuomo lived up to his nickname, "Hamlet on the Hudson," by spending months publicly vacillating about his potential candidacy before opting out in December.[16]

Overall, five candidates joined the race and stayed in through the entire pre-primary phase. Former Senator Paul Tsongas of Massachusetts announced his candidacy in April 1991. He took liberal positions on social issues while espousing a pro-business, budget-balancing approach to economic policy. Senator Tom Harkin of Iowa, a prairie populist who was the favorite of the labor unions, tried to reunite the old New Deal Democratic coalition. Senator Bob Kerrey of Nebraska, a former two-term governor and a recipient of the Congressional Medal of Honor for his Vietnam service, was touted as a candidate with the perfect résumé for the presidency. Governor Bill Clinton of Arkansas had been a founder in the mid-1980s of the Democratic Leadership Council (DLC), a centrist organization created in the aftermath of Walter Mondale's crushing defeat in the 1984 general election. Finally, former Governor Jerry Brown of California, who had made a late run for the nomination in 1976, jumped into the race as an outsider railing against special-interest influence in Washington.

By the end of 1991, none of the candidates had separated himself from the pack. Each had a major weakness in his candidacy that made the party hesitate. As a New Englander, Tsongas capitalized on the fact that his home base of Lowell, Massachusetts, was near New Hampshire's major media market. He spent a lot of 1991 wooing New Hampshire voters, and his poll numbers rose in that state. Nonetheless, it was hard for party members in the rest of the country to take his candidacy seriously. He had retired from the Senate in 1984 after being diagnosed with cancer. Now he had suddenly reappeared to run for president. Similarly, Jerry Brown had left politics in 1982 after completing two terms as governor and losing an election to the U.S. Senate. Neither candidate was able to raise much money or to draw early support from outside his home region.

Both midwestern candidates were also having trouble building national support. Tom Harkin hoped to use his home-state Iowa caucuses to catapult him above the rest of the field. However, few of the other candidates even bothered to campaign in Iowa, thus taking away any momentum Harkin might have gained from such a victory. Bob Kerrey's candidacy looked great on paper. Throughout 1991 he was seen as a candidate with great potential. However, he never was able to establish a clear message for his campaign and seemed to be uncertain as to why he was running for president. Consequently, activists were unwilling to commit to his campaign.

Of all the candidates, Bill Clinton appeared to be doing the best. From his days with the DLC, he had crafted a coherent message representing a "third way" that borrowed from both liberalism and conservatism. He packaged his program as a "new covenant," wherein government would form a partnership with individuals to help them become responsible for their own lives. Moreover, Clinton was a dynamic campaigner who was building a strong grassroots following. His big problem, however, was rumors of womanizing from his days as Arkansas governor. The party worried that his candidacy might collapse like Gary Hart's had in 1987, when similar charges became public.[17] As the 1992 primary season began, each candidate still had a lot to prove.

With Iowa's native son, Senator Harkin, likely to dominate the Iowa caucuses, New Hampshire's February 18 primary became the first real contest of the campaign. Only Clinton's campaign seemed to have gained momentum as 1992 opened. He was raising $700,000 per week and gaining the support of a broad spectrum of voters.[18] In mid-January, however, the Clinton campaign had to face its most daunting challenge—the candidate's past. Stories hit the newspapers of an Arkansas lounge singer who claimed to have had a decade-long affair with Clinton. When she held a press conference to play tapes of their telephone conversations, a media feeding frenzy began. In response to the charges, Clinton and his wife, Hillary, gave an interview to be shown on the CBS news program *60 Minutes*, immediately following the Super Bowl, when there would be maximum viewership. In the interview, Clinton admitted to having caused pain in his marriage but would not go into any detail. In early February, a new feeding frenzy began over stories about the extraordinary steps Clinton had taken to avoid being drafted during the

Vietnam War. The most damaging document was a letter he had written stating that it was important that he be placed back in the draft pool in order to maintain his "political viability." On February 12, Clinton appeared on ABC's *Nightline* program to answer those charges.

When the results of the New Hampshire primary came in, Tsongas, who had been campaigning there virtually nonstop for months, came in first, with 33 percent. Clinton came in second, with 25 percent, followed by Kerrey with 11 percent, Harkin, 10 percent, and Brown, 8 percent. Clinton appeared at his "victory" rally early in the evening, proclaiming himself the "Comeback Kid." Media coverage focused on how Clinton had survived the scandals to finish a strong second in a state outside his home base in the South. Clinton had shown that he could overcome the one major weakness that had caused Democratic Party leaders to hold back their support.

Over the next few weeks, Clinton became the clear front-runner for the nomination. He won many of the contests, and ran strongly in each of them. In nearly every state where he came in second, the candidate who placed ahead of him had a regional advantage—Kerrey and Harkin in the Midwest, Brown in the West, Tsongas in New England. Furthermore, Clinton's fundraising success continued while the others began to run out of money. Slowly, the other candidates dropped out of the race, leaving only Clinton, Tsongas, and Brown. After Clinton got over 50 percent of the vote in both Illinois and Michigan on March 17, Ron Brown, the chairman of the Democratic National Committee, began urging the party to coalesce around Clinton, at which point Tsongas suspended his campaign. However, Jerry Brown kept campaigning, playing the role of Grumpy by railing against the corruption of American government. Although Jerry Brown managed to win the Connecticut primary on March 24, the nominee had already been selected. Clinton had shown that he could build nationwide support, and had beaten the biggest rap against his candidacy. By mid-March, having survived a series of "scandals," Clinton had claimed the mantle.

Democrats, 2004: Grumpy Comes Up Short

The outcome of the 2000 presidential election enraged Democrats. On the morning of November 8, the day after the 2000 election, it was clear that the Democratic nominee, Vice President Al Gore, had received more popular votes than the Republican nominee, George W. Bush. However, nobody knew who had won the electoral vote. The unofficial vote tally in Florida showed Bush ahead by 926 votes out of 5.8 million cast. During the course of the election night coverage, the networks had first projected Gore as the winner in Florida, but later retracted that call. In the wee hours of the morning, they proclaimed Bush the Florida winner and the president-elect, but then retracted that call as well. Since neither side had yet won the 270 electoral votes needed to win, the winner of Florida would become the next President. After a month of lawsuits and recounts, the U.S. Supreme Court called a halt to the proceedings and Bush was declared the winner in Florida, which gave him an electoral-college majority.

Everyone assumed that Al Gore, whom many Democrats believed had been robbed of the presidency in 2000, would seek a rematch in 2004. Nonetheless, many Democrats were uncomfortable with sending Gore back into the fray. They believed that the Clinton record was so strong that Gore should have coasted into office. The only reason the election had been close, they reasoned, was because he had run a poor campaign. In December 2002, Gore unexpectedly announced that he would not seek the presidential nomination in 2004, throwing the race wide open.

Democrats were intent on beating Bush in 2004, but they were uncertain as to who would have the best chance of winning—or whether victory was even possible. Bush's popularity had soared after the terrorist attacks of September 11, 2001, and his successful military campaign to oust the Taliban government from Afghanistan. Moreover, Bush had defied history when his extensive campaigning for his party's candidates in the 2002 midterm elections yielded a Republican takeover of the Senate and enlarged margins in the House of Representatives. Bush's approval rating made Democrats skeptical that they could win the 2004 presidential election, yet their fury over the 2000 campaign drove them to try their hardest.

The year 2003 began with a buildup to war in Iraq. Most of the Democratic Party faithful opposed the war, but elected leaders were wary of opposing a popular wartime president on military matters. Consequently, the war in Iraq became the defining issue of the pre-primary phase of the campaign. Six men who were generally believed to be top-tier candidates entered the race for the nomination in 2003. Senator Joe Lieberman of Connecticut had been Al Gore's running mate in 2000. His ardent support of the war and moderate positions on some social issues placed him outside the mainstream of Democratic activists. Yet the name recognition he had gained during the 2000 campaign pushed him to the top of the national polls in 2003.

Three other members of Congress entered the race as well. All had voted to authorize the Iraq War, but had since voiced skepticism about its prosecution. Congressman Dick Gephardt of Missouri had been the minority leader of the House of Representatives for eight years before resigning that position in 2003 to seek the presidency. Gephardt was viewed as a party elder, having sought the presidential nomination in 1988. He had been a perennial favorite of labor unions, but many in the party believed that his time had passed. Senator John Kerry of Massachusetts was a decorated Vietnam War veteran whose policy positions fit neatly in the Democratic Party mainstream. Historically, voters have voiced greater confidence in Republicans' abilities to manage foreign policy. Kerry argued that his war record gave him the credibility to challenge Bush on his handling of the war on terrorism without being tarred as antimilitary. John Edwards was a rising star in the party after serving six years as a senator from North Carolina. His charisma, his southern drawl, and his uncanny skill at retail politics (obtained during his previous career as a personal injury lawyer) reminded Democrats of their last successful presidential candidate, Bill Clinton.

Howard Dean, the former governor of Vermont, was the strongest opponent of the Iraq War in the field. He claimed to represent the "Democratic wing of the Democratic Party," and sought to unite progressives and young voters in his cause. The last candidate to enter the race in 2003 was the retired general Wesley Clark, who had been President Clinton's supreme allied commander of NATO during the 1999 Kosovo conflict. Like Kerry, Clark emphasized his military record but argued that his Arkansas roots would make him a better general-election candidate than the Massachusetts senator.

Since there was no consensus in the party about what kind of candidate would have the best chance of defeating President Bush, Democratic Party and constituency leaders decided to take a hands-off approach.

Their plan was to see which candidate emerged from the field and then rally the party behind that person. However, they also wanted the choice to be made early to give the party plenty of time to unite behind its nominee. Consequently, the Democratic National Committee decided to allow states to begin selecting their convention delegates as early as February 1, 2004, instead of the March 1 date established in previous election cycles.

Throughout 2003, these six candidates jockeyed for position; none of them was able to establish himself as the overwhelming favorite. As the most conservative candidate in the field, Lieberman had trouble raising money from liberal party activists. As the year progressed and his opponents became better known, Lieberman's standing in the polls deteriorated. Kerry had a great deal of success raising money, collecting $29 million in 2003. However, his low-key campaign had much less success in winning the support of voters, and his poll numbers remained low throughout much of the year. Edwards had an initial burst of fundraising success, mostly from his fellow attorneys, during the first quarter of 2003. However, many Democrats were concerned that he lacked the political experience needed to be a credible presidential candidate. Gephardt had trouble shaking off the stigma of being a poor fundraiser from his 1988 run. Organized labor held back on an endorsement until it had proof that Gephardt could raise sufficient resources to run a national campaign, but without labor's help, raising money proved difficult for Gephardt.

Of all the candidates in the field, Dean had the most success in the pre-primary phase of the campaign. He bypassed the normal fundraising channels by using the Internet to tap into a large block of small contributors. By the end of 2003, Dean had raised $40 million and established an enormous national network of supporters. Dean's message and campaign style were of the kind generally associated with a candidate playing the role of Grumpy. However, with many activists waiting to see whose campaign would jell first, Dean's grassroots movement proved to be the largest organization in the field. As a result, Dean led the rest of the Democratic candidates in most national polls by the end of 2003. It looked like Grumpy might finally win a nomination.

Clark, because of his late start, had trouble building a substantial war chest and organization during 2003. As a fellow Arkansan, he was able

to attract a large group of Clinton contributors and campaign professionals, but he still lagged behind Kerry and Dean in both respects.

By the end of 2003, five candidates appeared to have a reasonable
chance of winning the nomination. Because of his success with Internet fundraising and his position in the polls, Dean appeared to have
the best chance of victory. His big fundraising advantage over the other
candidates led him to opt out of the public financing system. This decision eliminated both the national and the statewide spending limits,
and the Dean campaign poured money into Iowa and New Hampshire,
hoping to score an early knockout. His campaign manager began predicting that Dean would win every nomination contest, raising media
expectations to astronomical heights. Although Kerry had originally
planned to use New Hampshire as a springboard to the nomination,
his fellow New Englander, Dean, had pulled ahead of him in that state.
When Dean rejected public financing, Kerry did likewise. He lent his
campaign $6 million and escalated his efforts in Iowa, hoping that a
good showing there would boost him ahead of Dean in New Hampshire. Gephardt, a midwesterner, focused all of his efforts on the Iowa
caucuses, knowing that a loss there in his neighboring state would
doom his campaign. Edwards also focused on Iowa, using his skill at
person-to-person politics to increase his support at the caucuses. Because Clark was a latecomer to the race, he did not have time to build a
competitive organization in Iowa. Therefore, while the other candidates were campaigning in Iowa, Clark was in New Hampshire.

In the final weeks leading up to the January 19 Iowa caucuses, Dean
and Gephardt were airing ads that criticized each other as they battled
for first place. Meanwhile, Kerry and Edwards were slowly moving up in
the polls. One week before the caucuses, Christie Vilsack, the Iowa Governor's wife, announced her support for John Kerry. She was widely
seen as acting as a surrogate for her husband, who remained officially
neutral. Vilsack's endorsement brought with it the support of many local party leaders who had not previously committed to a candidate.
Now, Kerry had an enormous organization that was well schooled in the
intricacies of the Iowa caucuses.

The endorsement catapulted Kerry to victory in the Iowa caucuses
with 38 percent of the vote. Edwards came in a close second with 32
percent by winning votes the old-fashioned way—one handshake at a

time. The unexpectedly strong performance of both of these two candidates gave them incredible momentum going into New Hampshire. Kerry had come out of nowhere to win in a state where he had trailed badly only weeks before. Now he was headed back to his home region for the January 27 New Hampshire primary. Suddenly, Kerry was the candidate with all the momentum.

Dean's slide in the polls had begun about a month before the caucuses. Bush's approval ratings were declining, and Democrats were becoming more optimistic about their chances in November. They worried that Dean was too strident and inexperienced to be a strong competitor in a general election. His caustic response to the December 13, 2003, capture of Iraqi Dictator Saddam Hussein (which was completely at odds with the national euphoria) crystallized Democrats' concerns. Iowa voters, along with Democrats throughout the country, began looking for an alternative. Dean came in a distant third in the Iowa caucuses, with 18 percent. Gephardt came in fourth, with 11 percent of the vote, and ended his campaign the next day.

Kerry's election bounce from his Iowa victory moved him to the top of the New Hampshire polls, while Dean lost a great deal of support after his disappointing Iowa showing. Edwards also got a bounce, but there was not enough time in the week between the Iowa caucuses and the New Hampshire primary for Edwards to overcome his absence from New Hampshire in the preceding months. Clark, who had been campaigning nonstop in New Hampshire for weeks, lost ground as many of his supporters now saw Kerry, the other war veteran in the field, as a stronger bet to win. Kerry got 39 percent of the vote, followed by Dean with 26 percent, Clark with 13 percent, and Edwards with 12 percent.

One week later, on February 3, the candidates faced off in seven states across the country. Kerry now looked like a winner, and he was the only candidate with the resources to compete in all seven states. Edwards and Clark turned to the southern states to determine which of them would advance to the finals against Kerry. Dean's campaign collapsed as it became apparent that his Internet movement was no substitute for a grassroots campaign organization. He had spent all of his money but failed to build a firewall to break his fall. Kerry won five of the seven February 3 primaries, and Edwards and Clark each won one in the South. On February 10, Kerry won primaries in Tennessee and

Virginia, proving once and for all that he had support in all regions of the country. The party then rallied behind Kerry, who had obviously claimed the mantle.

Summary

Over the years, the transformation of one of the Seven Dwarfs into Snow White has happened much more quickly. Even though Jimmy Carter surprised everybody with his strong showing in the January 1976 Iowa caucuses, he was still battling for the nomination with the other Dwarfs until April. Likewise, it took Dukakis until April 1988 to complete the transformation. In 1992, Clinton wrapped up the nomination in March, and Kerry did the same by February 2004.

The major reason for the increased pace of this scenario is the front-loading and compression of the primary calendar. A candidate who gets a burst of momentum can ride it much further than in past years. After Iowa and New Hampshire, the candidates now face a flood of primaries. With no dominant candidate in the field, the voters in those states have little information upon which to base their vote. All they know is that one candidate has done well and the others have fallen short. With such limited information, voters are likely to take their cues from the earlier states that examined the candidates carefully and made their choice. This makes it easier for the first candidate who appears to be breaking from the pack to score victories in all regions of the country. In the "Seven Dwarfs" scenario, the race now goes not to the swift but to the first one to leap out of the starting gate after the bell sounds, opening the primary and caucus season.

Notes

1. Larry M. Bartels, *Presidential Primaries and the Dynamics of Public Choice* (Princeton, N.J.: Princeton University Press, 1988).

2. Robert Gordon Kaufman, *Henry M. Jackson: A Life in Politics* (Seattle: University of Washington Press, 2003).

3. Dan T. Carter, *The Politics of Rage: George Wallace, the Origins of Conservatism, and the Transformation of American Politics* (New York: Simon & Schuster, 1995).

4. Jules Witcover, *Marathon: The Pursuit of the Presidency, 1972–1976* (New York: Viking Press, 1977).

5. Peter G. Bourne, *Jimmy Carter* (New York: Scribner, 1997).

6. Kaufman, *Henry M. Jackson*, chapter 16.

7. Witcover, *Marathon*, pp. 165–66.

8. Ibid., pp. 199–200.

9. Ibid., pp. 187–89.

10. Richard Ben Cramer, *What It Takes: The Way to the White House* (New York: Viking Press, 1993), pp. 626–27.

11. Jack W. Germond and Jules Witcover, *Whose Broad Stripes and Bright Stars: The Trivial Pursuit of the Presidency, 1988* (New York: Warner Books, 1989), pp. 422–23.

12. Paul Simon, *Winners and Losers: The 1988 Race for the Presidency—One Candidate's Perspective* (New York: Continuum, 1989), p. 21.

13. Germond and Witcover, *Whose Broad Stripes and Bright Stars*, p. 219.

14. Ibid., p. 246.

15. Simon, *Winners and Losers*, pp. 23–24.

16. James Ceaser and Andrew Busch, *Upside Down and Inside Out: The 1992 Elections and American Politics* (Lanham, Md.: Rowman & Littlefield, 1993), p. 58.

17. Hart, who was the front-runner at the time, dropped out of the 1988 presidential race after photos were published proving that—in the middle of the campaign—he had spent the weekend with a model who was not his wife.

18. Jack W. Germond and Jules Witcover, *Mad As Hell: Revolt at the Ballot Box, 1992* (New York: Warner Books, 1993), p. 103.

6

Snow White and the Seven Dwarfs

IN THE "SEVEN DWARFS" scenario, we explored presidential nomination contests in which the winner is chosen after the primary season begins. In this scenario, no candidate so dominates the pre-primary phase that he completely overwhelms the rest of the pack. Instead, one candidate emerges after demonstrating his ability to win primaries among his base voters and perform well nationwide. At that point, party leaders rally behind his candidacy, transforming him into Snow White, and he is unstoppable.

By contrast, in a "Snow White and the Seven Dwarfs" scenario, one candidate is so dominant that party leaders rally behind him during the *pre-primary* phase. Usually this scenario occurs when someone is either the incumbent President or the presumptive heir to the throne. However, even if there is no incumbent or obvious heir, it is still possible for someone to achieve that status during the pre-primary phase. In either case, the outcome is the same—the party's nominee for president is determined before the first primary or caucus vote is cast.

Who gets to be Snow White under this scenario? A vital ingredient for claiming the mantle is raising money and building an organization long before the first votes are cast. Thus, if a candidate enters the race with an established national fundraising and organizational network, he can dominate the pre-primary phase. What types of candidates are likely to have such a network in place?

Sitting presidents and vice presidents have the ultimate advantage in this game. With the exception of President Ford in 1976, they have already won a national campaign. Thus, they have a team of fundraisers and organizers who are already loyal to the administration and want to maintain their access to power. Clearly, they will continue to support the incumbent. Thus, sitting presidents or vice presidents can rapidly build an experienced organization because they are not starting from scratch. Moreover, they can use the powers of their office to build support. As the leaders of the administration, they have had ample opportunity to do favors for various individuals and constituencies to attract their support. Moreover, as the presumptive nominee, the president or vice president has a great deal of leverage. He can win party activists over with a simple message: "I'm going to win so you had better get on board now!" Those who do not are likely to find themselves out in the cold, for other ambitious activists who joined the team early will have priority when the administration dispenses jobs and access. Also, presidents and vice presidents can command media attention any time they want it. These tools help them build a positive image that translates into popular support among primary voters.

Another type of candidate who has an enormous advantage is one who previously ran a good campaign for the presidential nomination but came up short. Such a candidate has built a fundraising and organizational network that can be reactivated. Since political analysts and party insiders view the earlier campaign as having been a strong one, these networks of supporters will be willing to try again. Thus, a large war chest and an organization can be built rapidly. Such candidates do not have as strong a position as does a sitting president or vice president because they do not have the tools of the office that allow them to do as many favors or get as much free media. Nonetheless, once they begin raising a lot of money and building a powerful organization, the media will take notice.

These advantages, however, will accrue only to someone whose previous effort was deemed a strong one. If, instead, the candidate did not do very well in the primaries, or the media found glaring weaknesses in the campaign, he gains no advantage for an upcoming effort. Potential fundraisers, campaign officials, and party activists will be well aware of the flaws in the previous campaign. Without overwhelming evidence that those weaknesses have been corrected, they will avoid working for someone they see as a sure loser. Thus, a candidate has to have run a very close second or performed way above expectations if he hopes to leverage his previous effort into Snow White status.

Finally, there is one other type of person who may be anointed the front-runner long before the first primary—the titular head of the party. When a party does not control the White House, it has to look elsewhere to find a leader. Often, this person serves as the party's leader in either the Senate or the House, and is widely viewed as its central voice in government. Other times, he is deemed the leading voice of an important ideological faction within the party. Although he has neither the inevitability nor the tools of the office that aid a president or vice president in securing the nomination, he does have stature. As the voice of the party (or one of its wings), he also has the ability to attract the media attention necessary to become widely known. If he uses that megaphone well, he can develop a positive national image that he can later translate into a dominant national campaign.

These are candidates whose institutional position has allowed them to become Snow White from the moment they launch their candidacy. They have so many built-in advantages that others cannot possibly compete with them. However, it is also possible that one of the Dwarfs, somebody not immediately anointed as the overwhelming favorite, can rise out of the pack to become Snow White during the pre-primary phase. To do this, he must excel at every stage of the game and leave all other candidates in the dust. He must raise far more money than the others, build a national organization, garner broad institutional support, dominate media coverage, and have the party rally to his cause. In 2000, George W. Bush became the first person to accomplish this feat. The Republican Party is sometimes known as the party of primogeniture because it always anoints the "next in line" as its presidential nominee. In the 2000 cycle, several potential candidates could plausibly claim to be the heir apparent. Bush convinced party leaders that he was the best candidate in that group, so they rallied to his cause. By the middle of 1999, he had so outpaced his rivals in every aspect of the pre-primary phase that he claimed the mantle early.

Now that we have identified Snow White, what can we say about the Dwarfs? They continue to compete with each other in the manner previously described in the "Seven Dwarfs" scenario. The field narrows to the final few. Sometimes, early in the primary season, one rises to the top of the pack. This Dwarf does not, however, transform into Snow White—that role has already been taken. Instead, he becomes Doc, the leader of the Dwarfs, who now must compete directly with Snow White. This is seldom a fair fight, however, since Snow White already has a massive campaign fund and an extensive national organization.

In most cases, Doc will defeat Snow White in some early state contests, making her appear vulnerable. However, she typically will have used her early resource advantage to build an impenetrable organizational firewall in states that constitute her strongest base. This firewall can break any momentum that Doc might achieve as a result of early victories. Doc, by contrast, is trying to turn his momentum into money and organization while he is also facing the voters in multiple states simultaneously.

The other obstacle Doc faces is heightened media scrutiny. The press can be a double-edged sword. While media attention can help an underdog candidate become known to the voters quickly, it also shines a spotlight on his weaknesses. When Doc was just another Dwarf, there was no reason for the press to scrutinize him. Now, as a potential nominee, the media expose the good, the bad, and the ugly. Thus, Doc must be highly skilled at media management. If the focus turns to his flaws, his momentum could be stopped dead in its tracks. Moreover, Snow White, who has already survived such a trial by fire, will be fanning the flames against Doc. Historically, Snow White has always managed to survive Doc's challenge because of her ability to build a firewall coupled with the media's heightened scrutiny of Doc. The Dwarf that pulls ahead of the pack does not win the nomination, merely the honor of being beaten by Snow White.

We should also note that the "Snow White and the Seven Dwarfs" scenario provides fertile ground for Grumpy. The voice of protest always needs a foil—an established figure to attack—in order to thrive, and having the nominee preordained before the primaries provides that foil for Grumpy's tirades. It is safe for people to vote for him because doing so has no impact on who will win the nomination. However, voters who are somewhat dissatisfied with Snow White might be able to influence her future behavior by supporting Grumpy. Knowing of dissension in the ranks, Snow White is likely to pay more attention to the wishes of Grumpy's followers. Thus, Grumpy keeps getting enough votes from his constituents to stay in the race all the way to the convention.

Five of the thirteen contested presidential nomination campaigns since 1976—four Republican and one Democrat—fit the description of Snow White and the Seven Dwarfs: the Republican contests in 1980,

1992, 1996, and 2000, and the Democratic contest in 1984. Four times, one party leader stood above the crowd from the moment he began his election bid. In the fifth, Snow White emerged from the pack of Dwarfs well before the Iowa caucuses. In each case, Snow White got a scare when Doc emerged, but defeated him once the primary season heated up.

Republicans, 1980: Snow White Cruises to Victory

The 1976 Republican presidential nomination contest had been a real nail-biter. The convention opened with neither President Gerald Ford nor former California Governor Ronald Reagan having secured enough delegate commitments to guarantee a first-ballot victory. Ford swayed enough delegates to win the nomination narrowly, but he lost the general election to Jimmy Carter.

As 1977 opened, Ford and Reagan were the two giants of the Republican Party, but Ford showed little desire to run again. In public statements, he said that he had no interest in pursuing the nomination but might be available should the party turn to him at the convention. Reagan, by contrast, wanted everyone to know that he planned to run again in 1980. After he lost the 1976 nomination, many concluded that the sixty-five-year-old Reagan had run his last race. To counter this perception, Reagan used the $1 million he had left over from his campaign account to start a political action committee to fund his political travels. He also went back to doing his radio and newspaper commentaries, and worked to support Republicans of all ideological stripes to reach out to party members beyond his conservative base.[1] As the only heavyweight in the race, Reagan was the clear front-runner.

With Ford sitting out the 1980 race, four candidates stepped up to fill his position as the moderate alternative to Reagan. George H. W. Bush had had a long career in government service. He had been elected to the House of Representatives from Texas, served as ambassador to China, director of central intelligence, and chairman of the Republican National Committee. His résumé was his claim to the nomination. Senator Howard Baker of Tennessee had won national renown as the lead Republican on the Senate committee that investigated the Watergate scandal. In that capacity, he earned a reputation for integrity and moderation that he believed made him an attractive presidential candidate. Senator Bob Dole of Kansas had been the 1976 candidate for vice president on Gerald Ford's ticket. Finally, Congressman John Anderson of Illinois entered the race as the most liberal candidate in the field. These four moderates were natural rivals, and one of them would have to defeat the others before turning his attention to Reagan.

The only major conservative candidate to challenge Reagan was John Connally. Connally had been a Democratic governor of Texas during the 1960s, but he served as President Nixon's treasury secretary and officially switched to the Republican Party in 1973. For the 1980 campaign, he refused matching funds and spent $10 million of his own money. He hoped to capitalize on the disappointment of some southern conservatives with Reagan's 1976 announcement that if he won the nomination, he would choose the liberal Pennsylvania senator Richard Schweiker as his running mate.

Of all the challengers to Reagan, only Bush seemed to have learned the lessons of Carter's victory in 1976. As early as 1978, Bush began traveling the country to build political support. He set up two political action committees that funded the 96,000 miles he logged traveling to forty-two states that year. He also began to build an organization in Iowa. By making multiple early forays into the state long before his official announcement in May 1979, he earned the support of all of the leading moderate Republican elected officials and party leaders. By the time of the Iowa caucuses, Bush had visited the state seventeen times. His campaign understood that he would quickly have to defeat the other moderate candidates so that he could be the lone alternative to Reagan. Without that, the moderate vote would be split among several candidates and Reagan would win.[2]

In the year before the primaries and caucuses, Reagan took a different strategic approach. He had already built a large support base during his 1976 campaign, and he reactivated that network of organizers and volunteers for 1980. His newspaper and radio commentaries, along with his public speeches, convinced his supporters to gear up for another race. So Reagan focused his time on building support in parts of the country where he had performed poorly in 1976, especially the Northeast, using his tax-cutting message as a means of winning over the voters. As a result, he spent very little time in Iowa.[3]

As the January 21, 1980, Iowa caucuses approached, Bush was the only one of Reagan's challengers who seemed to be gaining any traction. Because of his extensive campaigning in the state, Bush had won six straw polls in Iowa, plus one in Maine.[4] In a Florida straw poll, he narrowly trailed Connally for second place, substantially exceeding expectations.[5] When the Iowa caucus results came in, Bush had won with 33 percent of the vote to Reagan's 30 percent. Everyone else trailed far behind. Instantly, the media anointed Bush as Reagan's principal challenger, and his picture appeared on the cover of *Newsweek*.[6] Bush had become Doc, the leader of the Dwarfs, but the others remained in the race with enough strength to keep pulling anti-Reagan votes away from Bush.

Going into New Hampshire, Bush looked for every opportunity to transform the race into a one-on-one matchup with Reagan. An apparent golden opportunity arose when the *Nashua Telegraph* scheduled a debate for February 23 that would include only Reagan and Bush. But the Federal Communications Commission ruled that a newspaper-sponsored debate that excluded major candidates would violate its "equal time" regulations, so the Reagan campaign agreed to pick up the tab. Bush arrived at the debate ready for a showdown with Reagan, but Reagan outsmarted him by showing up with four of the other candidates in tow and insisting that they be included as well. In the verbal sparring that ensued, Reagan came across as a firm and decisive leader while Bush looked weak. When the moderator attempted to silence Reagan by shutting off his microphone, Reagan bellowed in his best theatrical voice, "I paid for this microphone." The debate went on with all six candidates participating. Bush's momentum collapsed and he lost the New Hampshire primary to Reagan two nights later, 49 percent to 23 percent, and the other moderate candidates picked up a substantial number of votes.

John Anderson, the liberal in the field, continued to receive a lot of votes. On March 4, he came in second behind Bush in Massachusetts and second behind Reagan in Vermont. Much of the rest of the field dropped out at that point, leaving only Reagan, Bush, and Anderson as credible candidates. On March 18, Anderson took 37 percent of the vote in his home state of Illinois. Thus, Bush was deprived of the head-to-head contest he needed if he was to have a shot at beating Reagan. On policy issues, Anderson was well outside the mainstream of Republican thinking, at one point saying that he would rather have the liberal icon

Ted Kennedy as president than Ronald Reagan.[7] Anderson was clearly taking the role of Grumpy—running to send a message rather than running to win. His transformation was complete when, on April 24, he left the race for the Republican nomination to pursue an independent campaign for president.

After his victory in Illinois, Reagan coasted to the nomination. Although Bush managed to win the Pennsylvania primary (where Anderson was not on the ballot) and the Michigan caucuses, there was no doubt that Reagan would be the nominee. On May 26, short on cash and with Reagan having won enough delegates to guarantee a first-ballot majority, Bush suspended his campaign. After an early slip-up in Iowa, Reagan had quickly recovered. The divided field ensured that no opponent could take him on directly. He had fallen short in 1976, but in 1980, Reagan claimed the mantle.

Democrats, 1984: Snow White Stumbles but Gets Up in the Nick of Time

After Jimmy Carter lost his reelection bid to Ronald Reagan in 1980, the liberal wing stood ready to recapture its dominant position in the Democratic Party.[8] Two men were the logical choices to be the instant front-runner for the nomination for the 1984 cycle. Senator Ted Kennedy of Massachusetts, the last remaining scion of the Kennedy clan, was a long-time liberal leader. In 1976, he had challenged President Carter for the nomination but had fallen short. His family background, his longtime leadership, and his previous presidential run made him a powerful potential contender for the 1984 nomination. The second heavyweight considering the race was Walter Mondale, Carter's vice president. Before being elected vice president, Mondale had been a senator from Minnesota whom many liberals tried to recruit into the 1976 nomination contest. When Kennedy announced in December 1982 that he would not seek the nomination, Mondale became the heir apparent.

The candidate whom the pundits considered to be Mondale's strongest opponent was Senator John Glenn of Ohio. Glenn had earned national acclaim in 1962 as the first American to orbit the earth. As a senator he was more moderate than Mondale, and thus could position himself as a more electable alternative for the November elections. Unfortunately for Glenn, elections are not run on paper. Unlike his space capsule, his candidacy never got off the ground. Mondale began attacking Glenn during a series of candidate forums during the fall of 1983, and it became clear that Glenn had not put together a coherent campaign message. Moreover, his campaign never built a strong organization among party activists. With no message and no organization, the Glenn campaign never got off the launch pad.

The year prior to the 1984 nomination contest was packed full of straw polls in states all over the country. These provided the various little-known challengers an opportunity to stand out from the pack. Lacking a strong organization, Glenn performed poorly in these contests, eroding his claim to being Mondale's principal rival. The candidate who seemed to do the best against Mondale in these contests was Senator Alan Cranston of California. However, as the Iowa caucuses approached, his campaign too seemed to be fading. His message consisted almost entirely of support for a freeze in the deployment of nuclear weapons, and as other candidates adopted his position on the issue, the rationale for his candidacy disappeared. Additionally, his support among the peace movement declined when George McGovern, who had won the Democratic nomination for president in 1972 as an opponent of the Vietnam War (but had gotten only 38 percent of the vote in November), entered the race.

As the Mondale campaign surveyed the battlefield, it saw enormous advantages. Mondale had earned the endorsement of organized labor and had enormous support among seniors and African Americans. In short, he was the darling of the old-time Democratic New Deal coalition. Moreover, the Democratic National Committee had created a new class of delegates for the 1984 convention known as superdelegates. These were elected officials and party leaders who were not bound to vote in accordance with the result of their state's contest. Most of them supported Mondale. Finally, the field of challengers appeared hopelessly divided and financially broke after a series of expensive and inconclusive straw polls. As a result, the Mondale campaign decided to pour a lot of money into early states to win a quick knockout and to begin preparing for the November election.

On February 20, 1984, the Iowa caucus results were not what the Mondale campaign had anticipated. Although the Minnesotan won his neighboring state with 44 percent of the vote, Senator Gary Hart of Colorado ran a strong second, with 16.5 percent, followed by McGovern, with 10 percent and the rest of the field in single digits. Hart had used his limited resources wisely, by targeting his efforts in rural areas where a few supporters could make a big difference in the delegate count. With his message of a "new ideas" Democratic Party no longer beholden to the "special interests," Hart had already built a large base of support in New Hampshire and the rest of New England. Doc appeared much sooner, and with a different face, than Mondale had expected.

In previous cycles, the front-runner had had approximately a month to mitigate any damage he might have suffered in Iowa before facing the New Hampshire voters. For 1984, however, the Democratic Party had decided to compress the primary season into a three-month window with New Hampshire coming eight days after Iowa. With his New England organization already in place, Hart steamrolled into New Hampshire and beat Mondale 39 percent to 27 percent, with Glenn taking 12 percent. Four days later, Hart carried Maine and Vermont as well. Suddenly, the inevitability of a Mondale victory was gone.

Even worse, the contest now moved to more states where Hart was strong or Mondale was weak. Nine contests were scheduled for Super Tuesday on March 13 (two in New England, three in the South, and five in Hart's home base in the West). Mondale had long expected to have problems with Super Tuesday because of the South's conservatism and its lack of strong labor unions. That was supposed to be Glenn country. Knowing this, Mondale had built a post-Super Tuesday firewall by encouraging Michigan to hold its caucuses just four days later, on March 17, leading up to a series of primaries in the industrial Midwest in late March and April. Now, however, having already lost so many contests to Hart, a poor showing on Super Tuesday could end Mondale's campaign before he could escape to the security of his firewall.

After Hart's strong showing in Iowa and victories in New England, the story line in the media changed dramatically. Instead of covering the unbeatable Mondale machine, the media now proclaimed that an unknown David was felling the mighty Goliath. However, as they introduced this new giant slayer to the public, some of the stories raised questions about his past. Although contributions came pouring into the Hart campaign, his team was unprepared for this media barrage.

Hart mishandled some of the negative stories, playing into the image of an untested, unknown candidate unready for the White House: he failed at the expectations game. Mondale, by contrast, was fanning the negative stories about Hart while simultaneously downplaying expectations for Super Tuesday. His winning any state, Mondale declared, would be a victory.

Super Tuesday also introduced into the game a new potential threat to Mondale: the civil rights leader the Reverend Jesse Jackson. Jackson was in all respects the prototypical Grumpy candidate. He had entered the campaign out of frustration, believing that Democrats were taking African American voters for granted. His anger boiled over during the 1983 Democratic mayoral primary in his hometown of Chicago. The field included two white candidates and one African American candidate, Harold Washington. The party establishment supported the two white candidates and abandoned Washington after he won the primary. (Washington won the general election but got only 19 percent of the white vote.) An angry Jackson ran for president, preaching that old-time Democratic religion, to send a message to his party. Moreover, he could potentially mobilize a large number of African American voters without spending a lot of money. Usually such candidates help the front-runner by further splitting the opposition votes. Unfortunately for the Mondale campaign, Jackson's base was in the cities and among liberal southerners, so a large majority of Jackson's support came from likely Mondale voters.

Mondale survived Super Tuesday only because he had lowered expectations so dramatically. He beat Hart in Alabama (34 percent to 21 percent) and in Georgia (30 percent to 27 percent), though Glenn and Jackson gained double-digit support in both states. Hart narrowly won Florida (39 percent to 36 percent) and beat Mondale handily in the other seven states. (Hart was not on the ballot in Hawaii, but Mondale still came in second behind an "uncommitted" slate.) In the world of reality, Hart had won big. But in the world of media expectations, Mondale had survived. At long last, the race moved to Mondale's stronghold, the Midwest.

There, Mondale started racking up wins. From mid-March through early May, he scored victories in large states such as Michigan, Illinois, New York, Pennsylvania, and Texas. These wins, combined with his large advantage among superdelegates, returned Mondale to a significant lead in the delegate count. Jackson earned double-digit popular support in these states, rising to 25 percent in New York, but it was not enough to keep Mondale from winning any of them. Mondale once again saw an opportunity to knock out Hart on May 8, with contests in Indiana, Maryland, North Carolina, and Ohio. Mondale believed that a sweep of these states would make him the presumptive nominee, so he campaigned in all four. Hart, sensing the same thing, focused all of his efforts on Ohio, winning that state along with neighboring Indiana.

For the remainder of May, Hart won a string of primaries and caucuses in western states, leading up the final round of primaries on June 5, anchored by California and New Jersey. Mondale predicted that after these primaries he would have won enough delegates to ensure himself a first-ballot majority. However, Hart won a larger-than-expected victory in California, forcing Mondale into a frantic round of phone calls to uncommitted delegates in order to obtain the promised majority.

Almost every conceivable factor went right for Hart, yet he came up short. The compressed calendar, with New England states scheduled early, maximized his momentum. Mondale did not build a strong national organization, relying instead on his union supporters, whose network contained important regional gaps. Moreover, Mondale set up his firewall in states whose contests occurred in the middle of the primary season—which was almost too late. If Hart had managed the media better, he might have won. What the 1984 Democratic contest illustrates above all else is just how many things must break the underdog's way if he is to keep the early front-runner from claiming the mantle.

Republicans, 1992:
Grumpy Stands Alone Against Snow White

George H. W. Bush was never a very popular figure in the Republican Party. He had placed a distant second in the 1980 presidential nomination race as the moderate alternative to Ronald Reagan, who then chose him to be vice president. Bush used that position to launch himself to the presidential nomination in 1988, despite concerns in the party about his leadership skills and his lack of conservative credentials. His first term as president exacerbated those concerns. Although

Bush had promised to continue Reagan's policies, his emphasis on "kinder, gentler" governance struck many conservatives as an implicit criticism of his former boss. The economy declined and the federal budget deficit soared in the first two years of Bush's presidency. A Harris Poll taken in May 1990 showed that 62 percent of Americans lacked confidence in his handling of the economy.[9] In late 1990, Bush infuriated conservatives when he broke his "no new taxes" campaign pledge during budget negotiations with congressional Democrats. The conservative base of the Republican party had moved from distrust of Bush to outright hostility.

In August 1990, Iraq invaded Kuwait and Bush sent troops to the region in preparation for war. After the successful expulsion of Iraq from Kuwait in the Gulf War of early 1991, Bush's popularity soared to 89 percent in some polls. No matter how uncomfortable Republicans were with his presidency, no serious challenger was going to take on an incumbent President who, as the 1992 presidential nomination season approached, seemed poised for easy reelection. Meanwhile, Bush was doing little to prepare for the 1992 campaign. A major reason for this was that, in mid-1991, Bush was uncertain as to whether he would even seek reelection. When he finally decided to do so, he told his advisers that he did not want to start fundraising until December 1991 at the earliest.[10]

As the Gulf War receded from the headlines, Bush's support among the public, and particularly among conservatives, collapsed. His public approval rating fell steadily (it reached a trough of 29 percent support in August 1992), and conservatives became more and more disenchanted with the Bush administration during 1991. Bush had not kept in close contact with the conservative movement since early 1990, when Lee Atwater—Bush's feisty 1988 campaign manager whom he had appointed to head the Republican National Committee—was diagnosed with brain cancer. After that, conservatives felt they had little or no access to the administration on policy issues. However, Bush's popularity did not fall to the point where he might be vulnerable to a challenge until the second half of 1991—too late for anyone in his party to launch a credible presidential campaign.

On December 10, 1991, Patrick Buchanan announced his candidacy as the one and only challenger to President Bush. Buchanan had neither the institutional nor political stature to be considered a legitimate threat to win the nomination. His previous government experience consisted of stints in the communications office of the Nixon and Reagan White Houses. Nor did the conservative movement consider him their leader. While they generally agreed with his views on social issues (the last straw that got Buchanan into the race was Bush's signing of civil rights legislation in 1991 that many conservatives called a "quota bill"), his opposition to the Gulf War and to free-trade agreements was anathema to most conservatives.[11] Above all else, Buchanan was a political provocateur. He was a newspaper columnist and a regular on political shout shows on television such as CNN's *Crossfire* and the syndicated program *The McLaughlin Group*. In short, Pat Buchanan was Grumpy.

In most instances, the number of votes Grumpy is able to win in primaries and caucuses is limited by the fact that there are other challengers in the race who appear to be capable of winning the nomination. In the case of Buchanan, however, he was the only Dwarf, facing Bush one-on-one. Thus, he became the vessel for Republicans of all stripes to cast a protest vote, secure in the knowledge that the party would never throw out an incumbent president and nominate a gadfly.

Consequently, Buchanan was able to effectively deliver different messages in different states. His first target was the February 18 New Hampshire primary. The economic recession had hit New Hampshire hard. Buchanan traveled the state extensively, advocating a policy of economic nationalism and excoriating Bush for his apparent indifference to the plight of the unemployed.[12] Buchanan won 37 percent of the vote in New Hampshire, holding Bush to only 53 percent. When the campaign headed south in March, Buchanan's focus turned to social issues. In addition to attacking Bush for signing civil rights legislation that conservatives opposed, he castigated the administration for allowing the National Endowment for the Arts to award grants to the purveyors of erotic art. On March 3, in Georgia, the southern state in which Buchanan spent the most time, he got 36 percent of the vote to Bush's 64 percent.[13]

Bush won every primary and caucus in 1992, building an enormous lead over Buchanan in the number of delegates won as a result of the winner-take-all allocation in most states. Nonetheless, Buchanan consistently won about 30 percent of the vote in the early primaries, dropping into the 20s later on. His support went well beyond conservatives; in most states, Buchanan did equally well among conservative and moderate Republicans.[14] As the only challenger in the field, Buchanan absorbed all of the anti-Bush votes, allowing him to do much better than a typical protest candidate. Buchanan served as a giant warning sign to Bush of the discontent in the electorate. That discontent manifested itself in November when Bush won only 36 percent of the vote in a three-way race, losing the White House to the Democratic nominee Bill Clinton. Despite his general-election loss, there had never been any doubt that Bush would beat Buchanan and claim the mantle.

Republicans, 1996: Snow White and the Underachieving Dwarfs

For the 1996 election, the line of succession in the party of primogeniture—the Republicans always had chosen the next in line—was rather murky. The Democrats controlled the White House so there was no incumbent president or vice president available. Nor had there been a serious challenger for the 1992 nomination, someone who would have become a natural heir to the throne. Whom, then, to select?

One logical choice would be former Vice President Dan Quayle. As George H. W. Bush's vice president from 1989 to 1993, Quayle had been the designated successor, but Bush's defeat meant that Quayle was not an incumbent, so he did not have the powers of the office as a means of leveraging support. Moreover, Quayle's tenure as vice president had been controversial. From the moment he was selected in 1988, he had been the late-night comics' favorite punch line. He had appeared to be "not ready for prime time," and none of his accomplishments in office had raised his stature in the media or with the public. Most Republicans believed that he could not win a general election for president.

A second alternative was Senate Majority Leader Bob Dole of Kansas. As the highest-ranking elected Republican official, Dole was the titular head of the party, and one of its most visible presences. Moreover, Dole had had a lot of experience running national campaigns. He had been Gerald Ford's running mate in 1976 and had sought the presidential nomination twice, flaming out early in 1980 but running a strong second in 1988. Dole had made it clear that he still had presidential ambitions, so when Quayle announced in February 1995 that he would not enter the race, Dole became the heir apparent.

Although his position as Senate majority leader made Dole a front-runner, his stature as a potential presidential nominee was not very strong among Republicans. His two previous performances raised a lot of questions as to whether he could run a competent general election campaign. Moreover, he was now seventy-three years old—Ronald Reagan's age when he started his second term. Many wondered whether he would be able to run a vigorous campaign and whether, if elected, he could handle the job for four years.

Given the inherent weaknesses in his candidacy, Dole was lucky that two men decided not to run, both of whom if they had run would have risen instantly to the top tier of candidates. In January 1995, Dick Cheney announced that he would not seek the nomination. Cheney had been the White House chief of staff during the Ford administration, held the Republicans' number two position in the House of Representatives, and had been President Bush's secretary of defense. Cheney's résumé and popularity in the party would have made him a formidable opponent. In November 1995, the retired general Colin Powell similarly announced that he would not run for president. Powell had served as President Reagan's national security advisor and had been chairman of the Joint Chiefs of Staff during the Gulf War. Since then, he had become the most popular political figure in the country, earning a reputation for independence, moderation, and civic-mindedness.

Ten lesser-known Republicans entered the vacuum created by Cheney's and Powell's absence. Two had the strong backing of their particular wing of the party. Pat Buchanan, a political commentator and former White House speechwriter, had challenged President George H. W. Bush in the primaries when he was seeking reelection in 1992. Buchanan criticized Bush for his economic policies and had become the darling of religious conservatives for his strident "culture wars" rhetoric during the campaign and in his speech to the 1992 national convention. Buchanan decided to run again and quickly gained the grassroots support of the religious right. However, his divisive style and economic populism made him an unacceptable choice for the rest of the party. During the summer of 1995, the publisher Malcolm (Steve) Forbes, Jr. began considering a run for the White House. A disciple of supply-side economics, Forbes was distressed that he saw no economic Reaganites in the field; he announced his candidacy in September 1995. His late start made it difficult to build an organization in time for the early primaries—to compensate, Forbes spent nearly $40 million of his own money on the race.

Two other candidates had gotten off to early starts in their quest for the Republican nomination. Immediately after election night in 1992, Lamar Alexander had begun planning his run for the 1996 nomination.[15] Alexander had been a two-term governor of Tennessee from 1979 to 1987 and had been chosen by President Bush to be secretary of education in 1991. In between, he had been president of the University of Tennessee. Beginning in 1993, Alexander replicated Jimmy Carter's 1976 strategy of touring the country to build grassroots support, with particular emphasis on Iowa. He also hosted a cable television program to build his national visibility. Alexander ran for the nomination as an outsider who knew how to get things done in Washington.

The other early starter was Senator Phil Gramm of Texas. In 1981, Gramm, then a Democratic member of the House of Representatives, had been a crucial figure in winning enough bipartisan support to pass President Reagan's budget, which contained substantial cuts in taxes and government spending. After switching to the Republican Party in 1983, Gramm was elected to the Senate and was chosen later to head the National Republican Senatorial Committee (NRSC), which spearheaded the Republicans' 1994 takeover of the Senate. Using the contacts he had made at the NRSC, Gramm began in February 1995 to raise a large campaign war chest for his presidential race, amassing more than $20 million by the end of the year. Despite his early fundraising success, Gramm was unable to win the full support of any major party constituency. Although he was a solid conservative on all major issues, his prickly personality and lack of charisma hindered his ability to gain constituency support.[16] In an effort to gain an early victory in the nomination contest, he convinced the Louisiana Republican Party to hold its caucuses on February 6, six days before Iowa.[17]

Four others announced their candidacies and stayed in the race until the first round of caucuses and primaries: Senator Richard Lugar of Indiana, Congressman Bob Dornan of California, former State Department official, Alan Keyes, and an industrialist, Morry Taylor. Two other candidates—Senator Arlen Specter of Pennsylvania and Governor Pete Wilson of California—dropped out of the race before the first votes were cast.

By late January 1996, serious doubts were growing among Republicans about the strength of the Dole candidacy. He had been given the task of delivering the official Republican response to President Clinton's State of the Union address earlier in the month, and his performance was widely judged a flop. Phil Gramm was now running a close second behind Dole in nationwide polls of Republicans, and Forbes had drawn even with Dole in Iowa and New Hampshire.[18] Moreover, Gramm had demonstrated the weakness in the Dole campaign by tying him in the Iowa straw poll in August 1995,[19] and running a close second in a Florida straw poll in November.[20]

The first delegate selection contest for the 1996 Republican presidential nomination occurred in the February 6 Louisiana caucuses. Only Buchanan, Gramm, and Keyes competed there—the others stayed away to avoid angering Iowa voters, who traditionally had the first caucuses. The Texan, Phil Gramm, had engineered the change, expecting to win his neighboring state and pick up momentum. However, since turnout was extremely low, Buchanan was able to mobilize enough of his supporters from the religious right to upset Gramm, 44 percent to 42 percent. Having raised expectations so high in Louisiana, Gramm's loss there torpedoed his candidacy. After placing fourth in Iowa six days later, Gramm dropped out of the race. Buchanan repeated his Louisiana strategy in Iowa, coming in a close second behind Dole. In the New Hampshire primary on February 20, Buchanan had reactivated his 1992 supporters and won with 27 percent of the vote. Dole took second with 26 percent, followed by Alexander with 23 percent.

Dole's candidacy was on the ropes. He had barely eked out a victory in Iowa, where he should have won big, and he had lost to Buchanan in New Hampshire. The following week Dole won primaries in the Dakotas, but Forbes won Delaware and Arizona after flooding the airwaves in those two states with ads attacking Dole. However, with the upcoming Super Tuesday primaries approaching during the first week of March, none of the other campaigns appeared to be very strong either. Buchanan had not broadened his support beyond his narrow hardcore base. Forbes had done well only in states where he had massively outspent everyone else. Alexander was touting himself as the only candidate who would be able to win in November, but the fact that he had not yet placed higher than third in any primary or caucus made his claim dubious. Nobody had been able to move ahead of the field to establish himself as Dole's principal rival.

Eleven states held primaries during the first week of March, including eight on March 5. Because of the weakness of the other campaigns, Dole won all eleven. No other candidate had the money and organization to compete with Dole in so many states simultaneously. Dole's performance reestablished him as the inevitable nominee, thereby crippling the other campaigns. Dole would not lose another primary for the rest of the year. By mid-March, all of Dole's challengers had withdrawn from the race except for Buchanan, who once again took on the role of Grumpy that he had played so well in 1992. He stayed in the race and got double-digit support in most primaries, but won few delegates.

The 1996 Republican presidential contest illustrates how much the field of candidates can affect the outcome of the race. Dole's position as Senate Majority Leader moved him ahead of the pack. He was blessed by the fact that no other candidate had managed to distinguish himself by the time the first votes were cast. If Cheney or Powell had entered the race, or if the campaign of one of Dole's challengers had caught fire in the pre-primary phase, Dole could well have lost. Instead, Dole claimed the mantle by default.

Republicans, 2000:
Snow White Emerges

After being out of the White House during the eight years of the Clinton administration, the Republican Party was looking for a winner. However, as the 2000 campaign approached, the line of succession had been hopelessly mangled. The Republicans had not had a president or vice president for eight years. They had nominated their Senate leader, Bob Dole, in 1996 and he had lost the general election. The Speaker of the House was new to his position, having just replaced a predecessor who resigned under an ethical cloud. For the first time since the 1970s-era reforms, Republicans did not have a front-runner two years before the presidential election.

In previous years, the line of succession had run through an earlier president and his ticket mate. From that perspective, one possible heir apparent was Dan Quayle, the Republican who had most recently occupied the White House as George H. W. Bush's vice president from 1989 to 1993. Alternatively, there was Jack Kemp, who had been Bob Dole's running mate in 1996. Or perhaps Elizabeth Dole, a former cabinet secretary who had made a strong impression during her husband's 1996 campaign. Sometimes, the heir apparent was a person who had run a strong race for the nomination in a previous cycle. In that vein, three candidates from the 1996 race could lay claim to the title: Steve Forbes, Lamar Alexander, and Pat Buchanan. In short, for the first time in three decades, the Republicans had a wide-open field.

As party leaders surveyed the landscape in 1999, they wanted most of all to find somebody who could win the general election. Their most visible elected officials were in the Congress, but the voters were disenchanted with congressional Republicans because of their unpopular impeachment of President Clinton in 1998. The strength of the party lay in the nation's statehouses, where a number of Republican governors had developed a governing conservatism that had proved very popular. But which one was presidential material? The most successful governors had no national prominence so it would take them a lot of time and resources to introduce themselves to the country. Also, they lacked the dynamism that would allow them to rally the party to their cause.

Eventually, one governor rose to the head of the list as the consensus choice of the governors. He came from Texas, the second largest state in the union. He had won the governorship in 1994 by defeating a popular incumbent Democrat. In 1998, he won reelection with 69 percent of the vote, and gained a higher percentage of votes from minorities than most Republicans generally achieve. And, of course, it didn't hurt that his name was George W. Bush and that he was the son of the former president.

Shortly after winning reelection to the governorship in 1998, Bush began laying the groundwork for a White House run. In March 1999, he started raising money at a pace never before seen in presidential history. Having watched Steve Forbes spend nearly $40 million of his own money in the 1996 primaries, much of it in negative ads against Bob Dole, Bush decided to decline public financing for his campaign, thereby freeing himself from any spending limits. By the end of 1999, Bush had raised $70 million.[21] In order to raise his national profile, Bush invited hundreds of party leaders, constituency leaders, and policy experts in small groups to meet with him. Each left the meetings raving to the media about Bush's abilities and his potential as a presidential candidate. With all of this positive press coverage, he rose steadily in the polls, far outdistancing his rivals. Bush dominated the pre-primary phase of the campaign in every respect, allowing him to rise out of the pack of candidates to become the prohibitive favorite—before any votes had been cast.

One of the remarkable features about the quest for the 2000 Republican presidential nomination was the number of candidates who entered the race but dropped out before the Iowa caucuses on January 24. Some left because they were unable to raise enough money to sustain a candidacy, particularly when compared to the Bush war chest. Others left after a poor showing in the August 1999 Iowa straw poll. With little money and no ability to put together a strong grassroots organization in Iowa, these candidates had no hope of victory. Of the twelve candidates who entered the race, six withdrew in 1999, including some big names from the 1992 and 1996 presidential elections such as Dan Quayle, Pat Buchanan, Lamar Alexander, and Elizabeth Dole. The field was cut in half before any votes were cast.

By the beginning of 2000, only two of the remaining Bush opponents still had viable campaigns. One was Steve Forbes, who had run in 1996 as the favored candidate of economic conservatives. In the intervening years, Forbes had succeeded in broadening his appeal by courting religious conservatives. As in 1996, Forbes bypassed campaign spending limits and spent $42 million of his fortune on the race. However, this time, Forbes had spent a lot of time and money building an organization in Iowa, hoping to use that state's caucuses to vault him to the nomination.

The second major challenger to Bush was Senator John McCain of Arizona. McCain had gained national prominence during the Vietnam War when he was held captive by the North Vietnamese for five years in the notorious prison nicknamed the "Hanoi Hilton." After being elected to the Senate in 1986, McCain developed a reputation as a maverick willing to oppose his party's leadership. For example, he had been the driving force for years in the effort to reform the campaign finance system.

As a presidential candidate, McCain had won over the press corps by giv-ing them unprecedented access. During campaign trips on the bus he named the *Straight Talk Express*, McCain would talk with reporters for hours about every issue under the sun. McCain had decided to bypass the Iowa caucuses to campaign extensively in New Hampshire. Bush, therefore, would have to take on Forbes one-on-one in Iowa and, if he succeeded there, take on McCain in New Hampshire.

Bush passed the first test by beating Forbes in Iowa, 41 percent to 30 percent. New Hampshire, however, was a different story. Bush had spent very little time in the state before the February 1 primary, whereas McCain had been there for months doing the retail politics that New Hampshire voters demand. Another advantage for McCain was that New Hampshire held an open primary; independents were allowed to vote in either one of the two party primaries. Bush was the establish-ment favorite but McCain was very appealing to independents. The only question was whether independents would vote in the Republican primary for McCain, or in the Democratic primary for former Senator Bill Bradley of New Jersey, who was running as an outsider against Vice President Al Gore. In the end, McCain got 49 percent of the vote to Bush's 30 percent, a stunning margin of victory that propelled McCain above Forbes as the principal alternative to Bush.

Over the next two weeks, Bush campaigned hard and spent heavily in South Carolina, hoping that a primary victory there on February 19 would halt McCain's momentum. Bush won South Carolina with 53 percent of the vote, but three days later, McCain won the primaries in his home state of Arizona and in Michigan. Again, McCain was aided in Michigan by that state's open voting; the Republicans were holding a primary but the Michigan Democrats had decided to hold caucuses later, in March. Consequently, independents flooded into the February Republican primary to vote for McCain. Bush appeared to be in serious trouble.

During this string of victories, McCain had been able to raise a lot of funds, mostly through small Internet contributions. Nonetheless, he still had much less money on hand than Bush. McCain could see op-portunities for victories in Virginia and Washington on February 29, but a week later, on March 7, was Super Tuesday, with primaries in eleven states. Most of the Super Tuesday contests would be closed primaries in which only party members could participate, therefore McCain could not count on winning the votes of large numbers of independents. Bush won both contests on February 29 and seven of the eleven Super Tuesday primaries, including the winner-take-all primary in California and the big-state contests in New York and Ohio. McCain was only able to win in New England. Super Tuesday gave Bush a large lead in the delegate count, ending McCain's hopes of winning the nomination.

Bush was the first candidate to so dominate the pre-primary phase of the campaign that he rose from the field of Dwarfs to become Snow White. After winning in New Hampshire, McCain had quickly earned the Doc role, clearing the field of all other challengers. He capitalized on the open primaries in early states to transform his strong outsider message into victories. However, McCain was so disliked by the Republican establishment because of his willingness to defy party leaders on important issues that he could not survive in closed primaries where only rank-and-file Republicans could cast ballots. After Super Tuesday, McCain lost all of the remaining primaries and Bush claimed the mantle.

Summary

Two major factors affect the level of competitiveness of presidential nomination races that fit the general pattern of Snow White and the Seven Dwarfs. One is the overall strength of Snow White's candidacy. Over the years, front-runners have learned that they must build an impenetrable firewall of support somewhere early in the campaign schedule to break the momentum a challenger might get from early victories. The compression of the calendar has facilitated this effort in that challengers must switch from small-state, person-to-person, retail politics to multistate, major media, wholesale politics in a matter of weeks, and wholesale politics cost a lot of money. They no longer have the luxury of month-long gaps between major primaries to raise money and spend it wisely. Nonetheless, Snow White has come close to losing when she has failed to build a strong enough organization in advance. The mantle is not given—it must be claimed.

The second factor is how quickly one of the Dwarfs rises to the top as Snow White's principal challenger. When one Dwarf has risen quickly and early, he has made the race much tougher for Snow White. However, in many instances, no single challenger rises above the pack in the early contests. Therefore, the battle among the Dwarfs for dominance continues well into the primary season and keeps the winner from turning his attention to battling the front-runner. In recent cycles, early fundraising has become more important and the calendar has become more compressed. As a result, if no candidate becomes the lone alternative to Snow White very early in the primary season, he has no chance of defeating her. The front-runner will have built up an insurmountable delegate advantage against a divided field. Thus, the recent evolution of the presidential nomination process has increased Snow White's advantage over the Dwarfs.

Notes

1. Lou Cannon, *Reagan* (New York: G. P. Putnam's, 1982), pp. 228–35.

2. Herbert S. Parmet, *George Bush: The Life of a Lone Star Yankee* (New York: Scribner, 1997), pp. 209–25.

3. Cannon, *Reagan*, pp. 235–37.

4. Parmet, *George Bush*, p. 226.

5. Elizabeth Drew, *Portrait of an Election: The 1980 Presidential Campaign* (New York: Simon & Schuster, 1981), p. 43.

6. Parmet, *George Bush*, p. 226.

7. Cannon, *Reagan*, p. 258.

8. This passage is a summary of the excellent account of the 1984 Democratic presidential nomination contest in Jack W. Germond and Jules Witcover, *Wake Us When It's Over: Presidential Politics of 1984* (New York: Macmillan, 1985).

9. Parmet, *George Bush*, p. 497.

10. Ibid., pp. 490–94.

11. Jack W. Germond and Jules Witcover, *Mad as Hell: Revolt at the Ballot Box, 1992* (New York: Warner Books, 1993), pp. 131–34.

12. Ibid., pp. 136–52.

13. Ibid., pp. 231–39.

14. James Ceaser and Andrew Busch, *Upside Down and Inside Out: The 1992 Elections and American Politics* (Lanham, Md.: Rowman & Littlefield, 2003), p. 41.

15. Bob Woodward, *The Choice* (New York: Simon & Schuster, 1996), p. 116.

16. Ibid., p. 111.

17. Iowa chose not to leapfrog ahead of Louisiana after most of the Republican candidates agreed to boycott the Louisiana caucuses.

18. James W. Ceaser and Andrew E. Busch, *Losing to Win: The 1996 Elections and American Politics* (Lanham Md.: Rowman & Littlefield, 1997), pp. 58–59.

19. Woodward, *The Choice*, pp. 240–49.

20. Ibid., p. 323.

21. James W. Ceaser and Andrew E. Busch, *The Perfect Tie: The True Story of the 2000 Presidential Election* (Lanham, Md.: Rowman & Littlefield, 2001), p. 68.

7

Clash of the Titans

Suppose a sitting president or vice president seeks his party's presidential nomination—such a candidate would immediately become the overwhelming favorite for the nomination. If others jump into the race, does it necessarily mean that the campaign will fit the "Snow White and the Seven Dwarfs" scenario? That depends on who challenges the favorite and how many get into the race.

In the "Snow White and the Seven Dwarfs" scenario, the clear favorite is challenged by lesser candidates (usually more than one) who do not have the capacity to jump quickly to the head of the pack. None is able to become the clear alternative until after the primaries begin—however, by that time it is too late to catch up. But suppose that a strong candidate with his own national base in the party mounts a campaign. The incumbent president or vice president now has a serious challenger with the potential (at least theoretically) to defeat him. We call this scenario "Clash of the Titans."

Earlier we noted that it is very risky to take on an incumbent president or vice president. He is the presumed nominee and has many powers at his disposal. For anyone, to have a realistic chance to win, the favorite must be seen as either ideologically incompatible with his party's base, not fully accepted as the leader of the party, or both. In this case, a major figure may step into the race to counter that perceived weakness. If the heir apparent is seen as ideologically incompatible with the party's base, a figure beloved by the party's true believers may take on the challenge. If a leading candidate is not accepted as the real leader of the party, the challenger is likely to be another party leader who can make a reasonable case that he should be the heir to the throne.

Either type of candidate has the capacity to run a national campaign since he has a large ideological or institutional base of supporters willing to join the effort. They are willing to antagonize the first Titan either because they believe he has betrayed the cause or because they think he is ripe for the picking. Whatever the motivation, the second Titan has a large and passionate enough following to raise money and build a national organization. He also has the stature to attract institutional support and extensive media coverage. Thus, he can take all of the necessary steps to claim the mantle during the pre-primary phase. There are no Dwarfs here—we have two Titans.

In every example of this scenario since 1976, one of the Titans has been the incumbent president or sitting vice president. While this is not a necessary condition for Clash of the Titans, the scenario has always played out that way. In most of these cases, an opponent has clearly qualified as a Titan the moment he announces his candidacy. Because of his stature as a party leader, he immediately establishes himself as *the* alternative candidate. He does not have to compete with other candidates for that honor.

However, we do have one example in which the second Titan had to rise above the other candidates first. The only prerequisite in the Clash of the Titans is that the second candidate must achieve that stature before the first votes are cast. This gives him the time and resources to mount a campaign comparable in scope to the incumbent's. In the 1988 cycle, Vice President George H. W. Bush was running for the top job, but he had never been popular with the party's conservative base, nor did he appear firmly entrenched as the heir apparent. Congressman Jack Kemp of New York, the author of President Reagan's tax cuts, ran as his ideological heir. Robert Dole of Kansas, the Senate Republican leader, mounted a challenge based on his post as the leader of congressional Republicans. Long before the first votes were cast in 1988, it was readily apparent that Kemp's campaign had failed to live up to its promise. Dole, by contrast, had raised a lot of money and built a powerful organization. Dole became the second Titan.

The Clash of the Titans contains the biggest question mark of all the scenarios. In every example since 1976, the incumbent president or vice president has won, and the winner was known well in advance of any primaries. In that respect we can say that in the Clash of the Titans, the voters are irrelevant. However, we do not have any examples in which we have two major party leaders running, neither of whom is a current occupant of 1600 Pennsylvania Avenue. If this were to happen, who would win?

The cases we have lend themselves to different interpretations of what would happen if neither Titan was president or vice president. Maybe incumbent presidents and vice presidents have always won because the power and majesty of the White House is uniquely overwhelming, so no other politician has been able to withstand it. In that case, neither Titan would necessarily have a clear advantage, so the contest could be decided in the primaries. Alternatively, it may be that the occupants of the White House win merely because their institutional perch is higher than any other. If so, in a case where neither Titan currently occupies the White House, the one with the higher institutional position in government would be certain to win because he would outperform his opponent in the pre-primary phase. Until such a situation occurs, we cannot know for certain which conclusion is correct.

In the meantime, we will examine the four examples of presidential nomination contests that fit the description of the Clash of the Titans. We will review the Republican contests of 1976 and 1988, and the Democratic contests of 1980 and 2000. In each of these cases, an incumbent president or vice president fought off a single heavyweight challenger to claim the mantle.

Republicans, 1976: The Great Communicator Challenges the Accidental President

Of all the incumbent presidents who have ever sought reelection, Gerald Ford had the weakest claim to his party's nomination. Ford had reached the presidency without ever having run on a national ticket. In October 1973, Vice President Spiro Agnew resigned under investigation for accepting bribes and kickbacks. Under the procedures established in 1967 by the Twenty-fifth Amendment to the Constitution, President Nixon chose to nominate then House Minority Leader Gerald Ford of Michigan as the new vice president, and Ford was confirmed by majorities in both the House and Senate. When Nixon resigned in August 1974 to avoid being impeached in connection with the Watergate scandal, Ford ascended to the presidency.

Because of the accidental nature of his rise, Ford did not have a ready-made fundraising apparatus or political organization. The largest election he had ever run in was for the congressional district of Grand

Rapids, Michigan. Nor had Ford, prior to becoming vice president, been planning to make a run for the presidency in the 1976 cycle—in fact, he had already decided not to seek reelection to his House seat in 1974 and so he had to build a national campaign from scratch in just two years.

Not having been the Republican Party's presidential nominee, Ford had never had the opportunity to unite all factions of the party behind his candidacy. Ford's reputation as a moderate who was respected by both parties was a major reason why Nixon had chosen him as vice president. Democrats controlled both the House and the Senate during Ford's confirmation hearings, so Nixon had to pick someone they would find acceptable. Republican conservatives, however, who had been activated by Barry Goldwater's failed presidential candidacy in 1964, and remained the party's most vibrant force, were not happy with Nixon's choice, and Ford made them even more unhappy when he asked the liberal New York governor Nelson Rockefeller to be his vice president.

Leading up to the 1976 election, the icon of the conservative movement was Governor Ronald Reagan of California. A former movie actor, Reagan had risen to political prominence through a nationally televised speech he gave in 1964 supporting Goldwater. Reagan had developed his communication skills during his movie career, and had honed his message as he traveled the country giving political speeches as the spokesman for General Electric. Reagan was as conservative as Goldwater but was able to present his views in a manner that was much more acceptable to the public. After winning the 1966 gubernatorial election, Reagan had served two successful terms as governor of California, which gave him the political stature and visibility he needed to be a plausible presidential candidate.

Thus, the stage was set for a nomination battle between Ford and Reagan.[1] Ford's initial strategy throughout 1975 involved convincing Reagan not to enter the race. His campaign hinted broadly that he would not keep Rockefeller on the ticket, and Ford's advisers met with Reagan to offer him high-level positions in the administration. Ford also gained the early endorsements of state party chairs in some of the large states, including New York, Pennsylvania, Ohio, and Michigan. None of these efforts worked. On July 15, 1975, one week after Ford announced his candidacy, the Reagan team launched Citizens for Reagan, an exploratory group that would begin raising money for a presidential campaign. On November 20, Reagan formally declared his candidacy.

While concentrating on keeping Reagan out of the race, the Ford team had done a poor job of preparing for a nomination contest. The campaign did not start putting together an organization in the first primary state of New Hampshire until September 1975, and by the end of the year, Ford had raised only $1.25 million. Meanwhile, Reagan was building an organization in New Hampshire, touring the country making speeches, doing syndicated radio and newspaper commentaries, and schmoozing with the press. By the time he declared his candidacy, Reagan had soared in the polls, surpassing the incumbent president.

With their backs against the wall and media expectations lowered, the Ford team finally struck back. Ford adopted a Rose Garden strategy, doing his job as president while his campaign team attacked Reagan. This allowed him to stay above the fray while his subordinates dragged Reagan down. They aimed their attacks at a portion of Reagan's economic program that would shift responsibility for $90 billion worth of federal government programs to the states. Ford's team, able to use the power of incumbency to gain the media megaphone, denounced the plan, saying that states would be unable to afford this plan. In tax-phobic New Hampshire, this meant that the state might, for the first time in its history, have to institute an income tax. Similarly, the Ford campaign publicized to Florida's seniors that Reagan was proposing reforms to Social Security. These attacks put Reagan on the defensive and stopped his momentum. Nonetheless, Reagan's organizers in those two early states continued to predict overwhelming victories, keeping media expectations high.

The New Hampshire primary on February 24, 1976, provided Ford with the victory he needed to jump-start his campaign—but just barely; he won by 1,317 votes. However, given his diminished expectations, the media billed this as a major triumph for Ford and a crushing blow to Reagan. The aura of inevitability that usually surrounds a presidential reelection effort, which Ford's campaign had lost in 1975, began to return. Ford used the momentum he gained from New Hampshire to score big victories in Maine and Vermont on March 2, and in Florida on March 9, where Reagan had once held a big lead.

Despite these defeats, the Reagan campaign was not dead yet. On March 23, Reagan unexpectedly won the North Carolina primary. The Ford campaign had grown complacent, thinking that Reagan was on the verge of withdrawing from the race. Instead, Senator Jesse Helms of North Carolina mobilized his powerful statewide organization for Reagan, helping him pull out a narrow victory. Now clearly back in the race, Reagan managed to win a number of primaries and build up a large delegate tally. He focused his efforts on states with open primaries and actively recruited supporters of Alabama's Democratic governor, George Wallace, to cross over. Wallace's campaign for the Democratic presidential nomination had fizzled by mid-March, so his voters and volunteers were eager to back Reagan as the most conservative remaining candidate in either field. Because so many of the Republican primaries allocated their delegates on a winner-take-all basis, Reagan was able to translate these victories into large delegate blocs.

On the morning of June 9, the day after the final primaries had been held, neither Ford nor Reagan had won the majority of delegates needed to guarantee a first-ballot victory at the Republican National Convention. A handful of states would be holding state conventions in the upcoming month, during which they would select some 270 national convention delegates. The Reagan team had prepared for these events better than the Ford campaign, but the party leadership in many of these states backed Ford. In this month-long display of old-fashioned bare-knuckles backroom politics, Ford held his own. After the state conventions, the *New York Times* estimated that Ford was only 28 delegates shy of a national majority, whereas Reagan needed 67 of the 94 remaining uncommitted delegates. Ford again used the power of his office, inviting these delegates to the White House for private meetings at which he secured their support. Ford went on to win a narrow first-ballot victory at the convention.

Reagan had a unique opportunity to deny re-nomination to an incumbent president. Ford had not been elected to the office and did not run a strong campaign. Reagan used his immense communication skills and the ardent grassroots support of the conservative movement to mount an extraordinarily effective campaign. Moreover, he used the rules of the selection process, particularly open primaries and winner-take-all delegate allocation, to maximize his delegate total. In the end, however, he could not overcome the massive powers available to any president, no matter how he came to that office. Ford had instant access to the media, the ability to do favors for key supporters and organizers, the capacity to claim credit for awarding federal grants to states and localities, and the imperial trappings of the office. When all was said and done, it was *President* Ford, not Gerald Ford, who claimed the mantle.

Democrats, 1980:
The Scion and the Peanut Farmer

In 1976, Jimmy Carter had won the presidency by campaigning as an outsider. The peanut farmer and former Georgia governor promised to clean up the ethical swamp of Washington in the wake of Watergate. He had won the Democratic nomination by going straight to the Democratic voters and, in the end, the party leaders had to accept him. However, the style that had served him so well in the election worked to his disadvantage as President.

Carter's term in office was plagued with economic hardship, foreign policy crises, and discord within his party. Stagflation wracked the economy as inflation rose to double digits (thanks mostly to shrinking oil supplies), while the unemployment rate increased. Carter was successful in negotiating a peace accord between Israel and Egypt, but the Soviet Union invaded Afghanistan during his term and Iran took fifty-two Americans hostage and held them for 444 days. At home, Carter struggled to get legislation passed through a Democratic-controlled Congress. He had the misfortune, as the political scientist Steven Skowronek has argued, of coming to power at a time when the Democrats' New Deal coalition had frayed to the point of tearing apart.[2] Having run as a political outsider against insider Washington, he had little ability to keep the various wings of the Democratic Party flying in the same direction. As a result of all of these problems, Carter's public approval rating fell to the mid-20s during July 1979, and polls suggested that the likely Republican nominee would easily defeat him in November.[3]

Massachusetts senator Ted Kennedy seemed destined to run for president at some time in his life. His brother John had won the prize in 1960, only to have his term cut short in 1963 by an assassin's bullet.

His other brother, Bobby, had been the front-runner for the 1968 Democratic presidential nomination when he, too, was assassinated. The question was not whether Ted would run, but when. He had seriously considered entering the race in 1976, but had backed out, leaving a wide-open field.

By 1978, liberal party activists, including Kennedy, had grown disenchanted with the Carter administration. Disputes over health-care policy mobilized their opposition to Carter. During the campaign, Carter had negotiated the text of a health-care policy speech with the United Auto Workers in order to win their support, and had pledged to move toward a system of national health insurance. As president, however, Carter seemed to place health-care policy far down his priority list, behind energy policy and deficit reduction. When he did make health-care proposals, they emphasized cost containment rather than universal access. Party liberals called on Kennedy to challenge Carter for the nomination, and created local Kennedy for President volunteer organizations in 1979.[4]

In December 1978, Kennedy's speech at the Democratic National Committee's midterm conference in Memphis was designed to spur Carter toward a more active effort on national health insurance. The Carter administration and the media took the speech to be a de facto announcement of a nomination challenge. Over the course of the next year, Kennedy moved closer and closer to a decision to seek the presidency in 1980. He was motivated not just by health-care policy but also by a general feeling that the administration had misplaced priorities and lacked leadership on progressive causes. Kennedy's speeches focused more heavily on leadership skills than they did on policy disputes. Moreover, Kennedy's drive also stemmed from a belief that he could win. Polls in mid-1979 showed him with a substantial lead over Carter among Democrats. In early September 1979, Kennedy informed Carter that he would indeed seek the nomination.[5]

The Carter team did not sit idly by while the Kennedy movement grew. In 1978, they crafted a campaign strategy reminiscent of the one that had proved successful in 1976. The four-part plan entailed starting early, expecting a serious nomination challenge, organizing to win everywhere, and spending campaign money carefully. As Kennedy's challenge appeared imminent, Carter began raising money and lining up endorsements from party leaders. The purpose of the latter activity was to deny Kennedy the momentum that he would have received from major party figures opposing the President.[6] As his potential candidacy moved closer to reality in 1979, Kennedy's poll numbers started to fall. His speeches were ineffective and the weaknesses of his candidacy became more apparent. Potential contributors and endorsers waited for some hard evidence that Kennedy could win before they would be willing to publicly oppose an incumbent President.[7]

Toward the end of 1979, Carter's approval ratings began to rise significantly as a result of greater success in passing his legislation through Congress. Then, in November 1979, Iran seized fifty-two American hostages, launching what was to become a 444-day foreign policy crisis. In December, the Soviet Union invaded Afghanistan. The public rallied behind Carter even more, as a show of support for their commander in chief. About that time, general election polls began to show Carter doing better than Kennedy against the Republicans, removing much of the rationale for the Kennedy campaign.[8] A Carter victory in an October 1979 Florida straw poll further stalled Kennedy's effort to raise money and build an organization.

On January 21, 1980, Carter beat Kennedy in the Iowa caucuses by 59 percent to 31 percent. He followed that up a month later with a victory in New Hampshire. A week after New Hampshire, Kennedy won his home-state Massachusetts primary, but Carter offset that by winning in neighboring Vermont. By this time, the Kennedy campaign was running on fumes, with little money or organization. Kennedy had one triumphant night on March 25, when he beat Carter in New York and Connecticut. However, the New York victory was as much a protest of a vote by the administration for a United Nations resolution critical of Israel as it was an endorsement of Kennedy. When the final primaries were completed on June 3, Carter had won enough delegates to lock up the nomination. Kennedy made one last effort at the Democratic National Convention by proposing a rule that would free all delegates from their first-ballot commitments, but that, too, failed.

The Carter campaign used the power of the presidency to starve the nascent Kennedy campaign of oxygen. By raising money and building an organization early, they kept the Kennedy campaign from building the necessary infrastructure. Potential Kennedy supporters, lacking evidence that he could win the nomination, were unwilling to defy an incumbent President. Once again, by getting off to an early start, Jimmy Carter claimed the mantle.

Republicans, 1988:
The Senator Versus the Veep

As Ronald Reagan's second term began in 1985, Republicans were faced with the task of finding his replacement. Reagan was still wildly popular in the party, so their task involved discovering who would best continue his legacy. From an institutional perspective, the logical choice to be Reagan's heir was his vice president, George H. W. Bush. Bush, however, had never been popular among conservatives since he had sought the 1980 presidential nomination as the moderate alternative candidate. Although Bush had served at Reagan's right hand for years, many Republican Party leaders were squeamish about giving him the nomination. He was a consummate bureaucrat, but they wondered whether he could be a successful leader. They also worried that Bush might lose the general election.

Two leading figures in the Republican Party stepped forward as potential alternatives to Bush. Each had a viable claim to being considered a Titan, but each also had serious weaknesses that raised warning flags for Republican activists. From an ideological standpoint, some thought that the logical choice to succeed Reagan was Congressman Jack Kemp of New York. Kemp had been the lead House sponsor of two of Reagan's major legislative achievements: the 1981 tax cuts and the Tax Reform Act of 1986. Moreover, his sunny disposition made him temperamentally similar to Reagan. However, there were serious doubts among conservatives as to whether Kemp was up to the challenge. They wondered whether he was capable of running a national campaign. As a member of the House of Representatives, he had never run for anything larger than his western New York congressional district centered on Buffalo. They also worried about whether his political résumé—that of a House back-bencher—gave him the stature to be president. After all, no sitting House member had been elected president since James Garfield in 1880, and he had been the Republican leader at the time.

The other major contender was Senator Bob Dole of Kansas who, as the minority leader in the Senate, was the highest-ranking Republican outside of the White House. A decorated World War II veteran, Dole also had extensive experience in national elections. He had been Gerald Ford's running mate during the 1976 campaign and had sought the presidential nomination in 1980. Paradoxically, Dole's national election experience was also his major drawback. He was widely perceived to have run terrible campaigns in 1976 and 1980. He had tried to be both the candidate and the campaign manager, unwilling to take advice from campaign professionals. Thus, his campaigns were highly disorganized, leading to his early exit from the 1980 field after faring poorly in both Iowa and New Hampshire. In early 1987, many Republicans were looking for an alternative to Bush, but neither Kemp nor Dole had earned their confidence. The pre-primary campaign of 1987 would determine whether either man was truly a Titan.

Bush got an early start in preparing for the 1988 race. At the beginning of his second term as vice president, he replaced most of his staff, bringing in more politically aggressive people who would help prepare him to run for President. Fearing a Kemp candidacy, he toughened up his rhetoric in an effort to mend fences with conservatives, making a special effort to court evangelical Christian leaders. He also traveled extensively to help Republican congressional candidates in the 1986 midterm elections, making 130 appearances in support of seventy different candidates. Bush's campaign staff began mapping out a strategy for how best to navigate the front-loaded nomination calendar. Bush's courting of conservatives was costing him support in Iowa, so his advisers decided he should focus more attention on New Hampshire. Bush traveled extensively to that state, meeting thousands of voters on every occasion. They also saw the Super Tuesday southern regional primary as an opportunity that only Bush would have the resources to exploit. His campaign built an impressive organization in the South, with special emphasis on South Carolina, which held its primary three days before Super Tuesday. They wrapped up the South so tightly that no other candidate could compete with them there, no matter what might happen in Iowa and New Hampshire.[9]

In the pre-primary phase of the 1988 contest, Kemp and Dole had to overcome the doubts of potential supporters about their campaigns. Kemp had to show that he was capable of running a national race and Dole needed to allow professional consultants to manage his campaign.

Kemp failed in the first task of any national election—raising money. Like all other serious presidential candidates, Kemp created a political action committee early in 1985 to fund his political endeavors, but in the first quarter of 1985, his PAC raised only $1.2 million, less than one third of what Bush's PAC raised. In March 1987, his campaign was already in debt.[10] With such a performance, Kemp demonstrated to conservative activists that he was not a Titan capable of defeating Bush. Dole, by contrast, addressed the concerns of the activists and pundits head on. He hired a group of well-known consultants to serve in the upper echelon of his campaign.[11] Then, he stepped back and let them run it. They called the shots and he did as he was told. Everyone could see that, this time, the Dole campaign would be different. It would be professional. Those who were looking for an alternative to Bush began to join the Dole campaign, believing it to be the only game in town. Thus, by the end of 1987, Dole had become the second Titan.

One other candidate demonstrated the ability to raise the resources necessary to run a presidential campaign. Reverend Pat Robertson, a televangelist and the son of a former U.S. senator from Virginia, mobilized his viewers to support his political ambitions. By October 1986, Robertson's PAC had already raised close to $12 million, mostly from small contributions solicited by direct mail.[12] This large mass of donors provided the manpower necessary to fund a national campaign and to build a grassroots organization. However, Robertson's grassroots approach also demonstrated the inherent weakness of his campaign. He had the ardent support of one segment of the Republican electorate—evangelical Christians—but no one else. Although there were enough evangelicals to have an impact in low-turnout contests, Robertson needed a much broader base to be nationally competitive. Also, direct mail is the most expensive fundraising method. It takes a lot to raise a lot, leaving little left to get a candidate's message out to the electorate at large. Robertson might have a marginal effect on the race, but there was no way he could win.

The first skirmish of the 1988 Republican presidential nomination process demonstrated the underlying weakness of the Kemp and Robertson teams, and Bush's inherent strength. Michigan Republicans had created a long, convoluted process for choosing their national convention delegates. The first step occurred in May 1986. The key to victory in Michigan would be the ability to organize and mobilize

potential supporters. Bush had the backing of the Republican establishment in the state, and Robertson had enough true believers to
flood some of the local conventions that began the delegate selection
process. Kemp had little money to spend on such a resource-intensive
effort, but he needed to do well in order to prove the viability of his
campaign. Dole, thinking that Bush would surely win in Michigan,
skipped the state to dedicate his resources to winning the Iowa caucuses. The Michigan campaign was a knockdown-dragout fight among
the Bush, Kemp, and Robertson campaigns. It was decided by closed-
door negotiations reminiscent of the operations of nineteenth-century
party machines. Robertson had a lot of troops, but they were amateurs
who were constantly outmaneuvered by the Bush forces. Kemp's team
negotiated with both the Bush and Robertson camps in an effort to
nail down a second-place finish. The Bush organizers were seasoned
professionals who were able to spend PAC money (not covered by
presidential spending limits) to coordinate with the state party's leadership. When the dust settled in January 1988, Bush had won 37 percent of the Michigan delegates, followed by Kemp, with 32 percent,
and Robertson, with only 8 percent.[13] Bush showed his strength, Kemp
survived, and Robertson flopped. But the other big winner was Dole,
who had used this time to create an impressive organization in Iowa.

The Bush team did not expect to do well in the February 8, 1988,
Iowa caucuses against a rural-state senator like Dole, but they could not
have guessed how poorly they would actually fare. Robertson mobilized
the sizable evangelical community in Iowa, a voting bloc that the Bush
campaign had been courting. Because turnout for the caucuses is generally quite low, Robertson made a dramatic impact. Dole got 37 percent
of the Iowa vote, followed by Robertson, with 25 percent, and Bush,
with only 19 percent. The sitting vice president had come in third in
Iowa. Dole's victory gave him a huge bounce as the campaign moved on
to the New Hampshire primary eight days later. Bush had built a very
strong organization there, but his embarrassing defeat in Iowa threatened to undermine his support. In the week between Iowa and New
Hampshire, the Bush campaign went into overdrive. Bush put multiple
ads on the air attacking Dole, who was unable to respond. Dole's campaign organization was under the highly centralized direction of his
high-priced Washington consultants, and could not adjust rapidly like

Bush, whose New Hampshire campaign was being organized locally by Governor John Sununu. A snowstorm the week before the primary demonstrated the difference in quality between the two campaigns. Local television news showed pictures of Bush greeting voters and driving a snowplow, interspersed with ads attacking Dole's record on taxes. Meanwhile, Dole was stuck in his hotel room while his advisers decided not to run a potentially devastating television ad questioning Bush's leadership ability. (The ad showed a snow-covered New Hampshire field that had not yet been touched by human feet. Its message contrasted Dole's legislative accomplishments with those of Bush, who for all his years in government had left "no footprints in the snow.") Bush broke Dole's momentum, beating him 38 percent to 29 percent, with everyone else far behind. The following week, on February 23, Dole won the virtually uncontested Minnesota caucuses and South Dakota primary, but got no surge of momentum because he had been expected to win these rural states handily.[14]

The primaries on March 5 and 8 proved to be the decisive battles. Bush had built his firewall in the southern Super Tuesday states, so he already had a massive organization there and had set aside a large budget for television ads. Dole's campaign, by contrast, had spent so much on consultants and high-priced professionals that he had only $800,000 for Super Tuesday, not enough to have an impact in sixteen simultaneous primaries.[15] In demonstrating that he could listen to the professionals, Dole had completely lost control of his campaign. Bush won every state on Super Tuesday and collected over 600 of the 800 available delegates. Dole tried to revive his campaign in Illinois the following week, on March 15, but it was too late. Bush had used the years before the 1988 primaries wisely, devising a workable strategy and implementing it. There never had been a doubt that he was a Titan. While Dole spent those years proving he, too, was a Titan, Bush stepped forward to claim the mantle.

Democrats, 2000:
An Old Pro Takes On the Machine

Al Gore had been preparing for the presidency for a long time. He had first sought the nomination in 1988, when he was just thirty-nine, and was defeated by Governor Michael Dukakis of Massachusetts. He opted out of the 1992 race but was Bill Clinton's surprise choice for the second spot on the ticket. Now, after eight years as vice president, Gore was ready to seek the top job again. As the sitting vice president and enjoying the enthusiastic support of President Clinton, Gore was clearly a front-runner for the 2000 nomination.

Nonetheless, there were some doubts in the party as to whether he would be the best nominee. Although Clinton remained popular, the final years of his presidency had been plagued by investigations into various scandals. In addition to his impeachment for lying to a grand jury, there were investigations into a number of financial irregularities, including charges that Gore had participated in illegal fundraising. Clinton's personal popularity had gotten him through his difficulties, but Gore did not possess Clinton's magnetic personality. Some Democrats worried that Gore would fall under the accumulated weight of the Clinton-era scandals. Knowing this, Gore tried to scare off any potential primary opponents by amassing large quantities of contributions and endorsements as early as possible. President Clinton gave Gore the keys to his fundraising machine and the money poured in. In addition, by the end of 1999, Gore had been endorsed by 500 of the 716 Superdelegates and the AFL-CIO.[16] Potential challengers knew that Gore had a huge head start in the nomination race.

One possible opponent with the stature to challenge Gore head-to-head was Missouri congressman Dick Gephardt, the House minority leader. Gephardt also had sought the nomination in 1988 and had since become a dominant figure among congressional Democrats. After the 1998 midterm elections, however, Gephardt announced that he would skip the 2000 presidential race in order to focus his efforts on helping Democrats regain control of the House. Since no one who held a leadership position in Congress was willing to challenge Gore, those seeking an alternative candidate had to look in a different direction.

One criticism many Democrats had of the Clinton administration was that it was too poll-driven; therefore, a statesman might be a good contrast to Gore. Senator Bob Kerrey of Nebraska fit that description. As a former two-term governor, a Congressional Medal of Honor recipient, and a serious legislator, Kerrey was widely acknowledged as a formidable political figure. He had sought the nomination in 1992 mostly because supporters said he should do so, but his candidacy failed because he never developed a coherent message. Although Kerrey considered running in 2000, he did not enter the race.

In September 1999, Bill Bradley, a former New Jersey senator, declared his candidacy. Before entering politics, Bradley, a Rhodes Scholar, had also been a star basketball player for Princeton University, on the 1964 Gold Medal-winning U.S. Olympic team, and with the NBA's New York Knicks. Like Kerrey, Bradley was widely viewed as a statesman during his eighteen years in the Senate. He had been the intellectual force behind the Tax Reform Act of 1986, which completely overhauled the federal tax system. He then turned his legislative efforts to finding a solution to the Third World debt crisis. In 1996, Bradley retired from the Senate, citing his frustration with the growing partisanship of the chamber. In announcing his presidential candidacy, Bradley staked out issue positions generally to Gore's left and decried the low ethical standards of Washington. Bradley quickly gained the support of liberal reformers and raised enough money by the end of 1999 to be competitive with Gore.[17]

Bradley rose quickly in the national polls and moved ahead of Gore in New Hampshire. Now that Gore had a challenger, his campaign moved into the attack mode. Gore picked apart Bradley's health-care proposals, assailing them as both too expensive and not sufficiently comprehensive. He also criticized Bradley for retiring from the Senate after the Republicans had taken control of Congress in 1994, saying that Bradley should have stayed to fight against their conservative agenda. In debates, Gore's tenacious style kept Bradley on the defensive.

Having moved ahead of Gore in New Hampshire polls, Bradley decided that he should also try to win the January 24 Iowa caucuses. He believed that victories in both states would knock Gore out of the race. However, Gore had already built a strong organization in Iowa that would be very difficult for Bradley to overcome given the usual low turnout for caucuses. Gore won the Iowa caucuses with 63 percent of the vote to Bradley's 35 percent. Although Bradley had tried to tamp down expectations in the final days of the Iowa campaign, the media portrayed the result as a big win for Gore.

Now, Bradley faced an unexpected problem as he looked to rebound in the February 1 New Hampshire primary. Since Gore was the favorite of the Democratic Party establishment, Bradley had planned to win the votes of independents in New Hampshire's open primary. However, on the Republican side of the nomination battle, Senator John McCain's outsider strategy was identical to Bradley's. While Bradley was on the defensive against Gore, McCain was on offense against the Republican establishment's favorite, George W. Bush, who had spent little time campaigning in New Hampshire. Independents were forced to choose whether to vote in the Democratic or Republican primary. On election day, most independent voters opted for McCain over Bradley. Bradley narrowly lost to Gore, 50 percent to 46 percent, while McCain defeated Bush handily. Instead of winning Iowa and New Hampshire as he had planned, Bradley lost them both.

In the previous three presidential nomination cycles, a large number of primaries and caucuses had been held in the weeks immediately following the New Hampshire primary. That was not the case for the Democrats in 2000. The Democratic National Committee had decided to continue its practice from previous cycles of setting March 1 as the first date that states other than Iowa and New Hampshire would be allowed to hold their presidential nomination contests. The Republicans, however, had advanced their own opening date to February 1, 2000. Thus, many states moved their Republican primaries to February, forcing Iowa and New Hampshire to move their dates forward as well to maintain their "first-in-the-nation" status. Since the Democrats would not accept delegates chosen in February, the "February primary" states held separate Democratic contests later in the spring. Thus, the calendar for the 2000 Democratic presidential nomination race had a gaping hole between the New Hampshire primary on February 1 and the Super Tuesday primaries on March 7.

With no Democratic contests to report on during February, the media turned its entire attention to the Republicans. Bradley, having lost in both Iowa and New Hampshire, was unable to get the media coverage he needed to claw back into the race. Having lost all of the momentum he had gained in 1999, Bradley lost all eleven Super Tuesday primaries to Gore on March 7, 2000. Bradley was no longer viewed as a viable candidate and the party coalesced around Gore. Bradley had fallen into a black hole as Gore claimed the mantle.

Summary

Presidential nomination battles that fit the general description of the Clash of the Titans have grown increasingly uncompetitive over the years. In 1976, Ronald Reagan battled Gerald Ford all the way to the convention in August. In 1980, Jimmy Carter did not clinch the nomination over Ted Kennedy until June. In 1988, George H. W. Bush disposed of Bob Dole in mid-March. In 2000, the Al Gore–Bill Bradley race was over in early March when Gore swept the Super Tuesday contests. The cause of this trend is not simply the front-loading of the calendar; these races have concluded after progressively fewer contests have been held.

It is somewhat difficult to generalize about the "Clash of the Titans" scenario, since every winner has been either an incumbent president or a sitting vice president. Nonetheless, it is worth noting that the quality of the second Titan has dropped since 1980. Reagan (1976) and Kennedy (1980) were the undisputed leaders of the opposition wing of their parties when they sought the nomination. They were instant Titans. By 1988, Dole had to defeat Jack Kemp in the pre-primary phase before he could focus exclusively on Bush. And in 2000, Bradley was (at best) the third choice of Gore opponents.

What remains unclear, however, is the precise cause of this declining competitiveness. One possibility is enhanced incumbent advantage. At all levels of government, incumbency advantage has grown as office holders have mastered the art of using the perks of office to gain electoral advantage. Presidents and vice presidents can use the power of the White House more than ever before to reward their supporters and punish their opponents. Challengers know this and are therefore understandably unwilling to take on the White House if they hope to have a political future. Alternatively, it could be the case that the front-loading of primaries and the growing importance of money have allowed the better candidate to overwhelm his opponent more quickly. We will not be able to judge these two hypotheses until we have a clash between two nonincumbent Titans. Until then, we can see that the Clash of the Titans has become a much shorter game, just like the other two scenarios.

Notes

1. This section is based on the excellent account of the 1976 Republican presidential nomination in Jules Witcover, *Marathon: The Pursuit of the Presidency, 1972–1976* (New York: Viking Press, 1977).

2. Steven Skowronek, *The Politics Presidents Make: Leadership from John Adams to George Bush* (Cambridge, Mass.: Belknap Press of Harvard University Press, 1997).

3. Peter G. Bourne, *Jimmy Carter* (New York: Scribner, 1997), p. 445.

4. Ibid., pp. 432–36.

5. Adam Clymer, *Edward M. Kennedy: A Biography* (New York: HarperPerennial, 1999), pp. 276–84.

6. Elizabeth Drew, *Portrait of an Election: The 1980 Presidential Campaign* (New York: Simon & Schuster, 1981), pp. 123–25.

7. Ibid., pp. 18–20.

8. Clymer, *Edward M. Kennedy*, pp. 298–99.

9. Herbert S. Parmet, *George Bush: The Life of a Lone Star Yankee* (New York: Scribner, 1997), pp. 301–9.

10. Jack W. Germond and Jules Witcover, *Whose Broad Stripes and Bright Stars: The Trivial Pursuit of the Presidency 1988* (New York: Warner Books, 1989), pp. 73–77.

11. Richard Ben Cramer, *What It Takes: The Way to the White House* (New York: Vintage Books, 1993).

12. Germond and Witcover, *Whose Broad Stripes and Bright Stars*, p. 73.

13. Ibid., pp. 81–100.

14. Germond and Witcover, *Whose Broad Stripes and Bright Stars*, pp. 137–47.

15. Cramer, *What It Takes*, p. 902.

16. James W. Ceaser and Andrew E. Busch, *The Perfect Tie: The True Story of the 2000 Presidential Election* (Lanham, Md.: Rowman & Littlefield, 2001), p. 72.

17. Ibid., p. 72.

8

Looking Ahead

W HEN FUTURE SCHOLARS LOOK back at the 2004 presidential nomination contest, they may see it as a transformational year. The modern system by which parties choose their presidential candidates began with the 1970s reforms of the delegate-selection process and the campaign finance system. Both of these systems have evolved in ways that undercut the original intent of the reformers—the law of unintended consequences in action. In 2004, the front-loading and compression of the primary calendar nearly led to the nomination of a very weak general election candidate, Howard Dean. We also witnessed the collapse of the system of partial public financing paired with spending limits.

We have examined how the system got to its present form, looking at the system's original design and how it created an incentive structure that led the various players to adopt strategies that would maximize their goals. The result has been a straight-line march to an accelerated process in which candidates raise as much money as possible as early as possible. Those developments appear to have reached the end of the line; future adjustments, if they are to occur, will have to veer off in a different direction. What direction might that be? What obstacles stand in the way of reform? And is the system really broken? These are the questions we will address in this concluding chapter.

Reforming the Calendar

The principal goal of the 1970 McGovern-Fraser Commission reforms was to democratize the process of selecting the party's presidential nominee by eliminating the complete control that state party leaders had over their national convention delegations. States were required to choose their delegates through a transparent process—a primary or a convention—that resulted in a delegation that reflected the views of party members. Over the years, state parties began scheduling their con-tests earlier and earlier to maximize the influence of their state on the choice of a candidate. In 2004, national party leaders enhanced the trend because they wanted a nominee to be chosen very early in order to give the party time to unite behind the winner. A primary season that originally lasted for over four months had been compressed into two months, with the outcome generally determined in the first month.

An implicit goal of the commission was to create a process that would yield a nominee with a good chance of winning in November. By 1984, Democratic Party officials were already worried that the new sys-tem favored outsiders who would not run strong general election cam-paigns. To resolve this problem, they added superdelegates—party leaders as convention delegates who would not be bound by their state's primary results; this, they felt, would contribute to choosing a strong candidate who could win. In fact, after 1984, outsiders no longer won—but this was not due to the addition of superdelegates. Outsider candi-dates had won previous nominations not because the system favored them but because they had been the only ones in the field who knew how to work the system. By 1984, everyone knew the best strategies.

We have examined the three scenarios ("Seven Dwarfs," "Snow White and the Seven Dwarfs," and "Clash of the Titans") that explain the last thirteen contested presidential nominations. Does the current system live up to the twin goals of democratizing the nomination sys-tem and also choosing a viable candidate? With the incredible front-loading and compression of the primary season in recent cycles, none of the scenarios lives up to the democratic aspirations of the original reformers. The voters affect the outcome of the nomination process only when no candidate has dominated the pre-primary phase. More-over, in such instances, voter impact is limited to the handful of states that have very early contests because the nominee is chosen so quickly.

Nonetheless, the two parties had been generally satisfied over the years with the caliber of the candidate who emerged as the nominee. In 2004, however, the system came very close to yielding a candidate who had no possibility of winning the general election. Howard Dean har-nessed the passion of the antiwar movement and nearly won the nom-ination in a year in which the Democratic establishment was divided over what kind of nominee it wanted. Dean's candidacy began to self-destruct about a month before the Iowa caucuses, leaving enough time for the party to find an alternative they believed would be more competitive in November. Had Dean held on for another two months, he probably would have won the nomination. Although this would not have been the first time that such a weak candidate had won the nomination, it would have been the most troublesome. George McGovern had won the 1972 Democratic presidential nomination because, as the chairman of the committee that wrote the new rules, he was the only candidate in the field who really understood them. The problem was self-correcting once everyone else caught on. The Dean case, however, suggests a systemic flaw. In a "Seven Dwarfs" scenario, combined with a compressed calendar, the parties run the risk of nominating a sure loser. For this reason, it is likely that the schedule will not be allowed to become more front-loaded than it currently is.

Every four years, after watching the parties choose their presidential nominees, reformers bemoan the fact that the voters in Iowa and New Hampshire appear to have inordinate influence over the selection process. They begin proposing alternative systems that they believe would distribute power more fairly. One option is to have a national primary, with all party members voting on the same day. This, they argue, would ensure that the calendar has no impact on the distribution of power. A second oft-discussed option is to have a series of regional primaries. The schedule would separate the primaries by several weeks to give candidates an opportunity to campaign across the region, and the order would be rotated every cycle to ensure that no single region always went first.

In theory, either of these options would allow voters from across the country to have a voice in the selection their party's presidential nominee. However, in reality, they would only make the problem worse. Right from the start, the candidates would have to compete in a large number of states simultaneously. To do so effectively, the candidate would need enough money to purchase television ads across the region or the entire country. Thus, the candidate who has raised the most money and built the strongest organization in the pre-primary phase would have an even greater advantage. The Jimmy Carter strategy— leveraging the momentum from a victory in the earliest contest into a rapid growth in money and organization—would be precluded. The pre-primary phase would be even more determinative than it is under the current system.

An alternative approach favored by some reformers is the creation of a centrally planned, graduated schedule. The general idea is that primaries would be held only on selected days spread evenly throughout the primary season. States would be assigned to hold their contest on a specified date. The resulting schedule would begin with a few small state contests, with each succeeding primary date selecting a progressively larger number of delegates. Such a plan gives underdogs a chance to utilize the Carter strategy while increasing the likelihood that late primaries will still affect the outcome of the race.

Any such system, however, faces an important political problem. States would have to agree to surrender their right to schedule their primaries as they see fit. State party leaders are likely to balk at surrendering their last remaining mechanism for maximizing their influence in the selection process. Another practical problem stems from the fact that many states want to hold their congressional primary on the same day as the presidential primary, in order to save money. Any centrally planned system would force states either to separate the two or surrender the scheduling of their congressional primaries as well. Moreover, the two parties would have to agree on any such system because state law determines the date of primaries in most states. Many state legislatures would be unwilling to abide by a plan designed for only one party.

Front-loading may have reached its limits. The Democratic Party's narrow escape in 2004 makes it unlikely that the problem will become more pronounced. It may even create a stronger movement to overhaul the delegate-selection system. However, any such efforts would have to overcome the desire of state party leaders to maximize their power and of national party leaders to select a nominee as early as possible.

Reforming the Presidential Campaign Finance System

The Federal Election Campaign Act amendments of 1974 created a voluntary system of public financing and spending limits for presidential elections. Candidates who agreed to limit the amount of money they spent to win the presidential nomination would receive partial matching funds from the U.S. Treasury. Until 1996, no candidate who had opted out of the voluntary system had run a competitive race for the nomination. In 1996, Steve Forbes turned down the matching funds so that he could spend an unlimited amount of his own money in his quest for the Republican nomination. He outspent his opponents and won two state primaries. In 2000, George W. Bush also opted out of the system and his campaign raised $100 million, over twice as much as any of his rivals. In 2004, Democrats John Kerry and Howard Dean rejected the spending limits, as did Bush, who ran unopposed for the Republican nomination. The two nominees, Kerry and Bush, raised nearly $400 million combined from January 2003 through June 2004. It is unlikely that any future presidential nominee will accept public funding and spending limits during the primaries.

Three factors have intervened to make the public funding system unattractive for any nominee. One was the doubling of the individual contribution limit in the Bipartisan Campaign Reform Act, which was enacted in 2002. This made it easier for campaigns to raise large sums of money. It also lessened the importance of matching funds, whose upper limits were not affected by BCRA, because they now represented a smaller percentage of the maximum individual contribution.

The second was the fact that successful candidates did not have to worry anymore about being able to raise enough money after wrapping up the nomination to hold them over until their nominating convention. The country has become highly polarized and evenly divided. This has increased the political cost for party activists of losing the presidency. It has also virtually guaranteed that presidential elections will be close. No matter whom they supported in the primaries, activists will contribute to the party's nominee once he emerges from the field. And 2004 showed us that there is an immense amount of political money to be raised.

Third, the candidates know that they will be vastly outspent in the run-up to the party conventions if they accept spending limits. Thus, accepting public financing in their quest for the nomination will cripple their ability to win the general election. Consequently, it is likely that all major candidates will opt out of the system during the primaries. The breakdown of the public financing system for presidential nominations serves to increase the front-runner's advantage even more. Since the spending limits and matching funds level the playing field between the candidates, their absence means that those who can raise the most money will have an even greater advantage than they do at present. This puts a greater premium on the pre-primary phase of the campaign, making the voters even less important than they are now.

Since the passage of the Bipartisan Campaign Reform Act, reformers have begun to examine ways to reform the presidential campaign finance system. In order to encourage candidates to stay within the FECA system, reformers are seeking to make matching funds a more important part of the overall fundraising mix. To achieve this goal, they are seeking to increase the amount of matching funds for which a campaign is eligible. Specific proposals include raising the threshold below which contributions can be matched and increasing the percentage of the match to some multiple of the contribution. To deal with the problem of candidates' having insufficient funds to cover the entire period between the first primary and the convention, reformers have proposed increasing a candidate's overall spending limit for the primaries to match the general election limit. In this way, campaigns would be less likely to spend all of their money months before the convention.

Both of these solutions, however, require a lot more public money. Where will the funds come from? The Presidential Election Fund is already struggling to keep up with demand; its revenues have fallen because people have become less willing to contribute. Increasing the amount of public money campaigns could receive would surely bankrupt the system unless a source for an infusion of new money is found. Consequently, some reformers are proposing that taxpayers be allowed to designate an amount larger than the current $3 for the fund each year. Others propose that money from the U.S. Treasury's general revenue fund be used as a supplement if needed. Thus, reformers are running into the problem that shoring up the current public financing system will require a lot of public money that does not currently exist and will be difficult to find.

Is This Any Way to Select a President?

In 1888, James Bryce, a British aristocrat, published an extensive study of American political institutions, *The American Commonwealth*. His book contained a chapter on presidential elections, "Why Great Men Are Not Chosen Presidents," in which his core argument was that the process whereby parties choose their candidates precludes the selection of statesmen. At the time, presidential nominees were chosen by state party leaders who gathered in smoke-filled rooms at the national conventions. After much discussion, they would find a consensus candidate who was acceptable to all of them. In order to be a presidential nominee, therefore, you had to have made no enemies. Consequently, in the latter part of the nineteenth century, the parties chose mediocrities whose principal qualification was that they had offended no one.

In effect, Bryce was arguing that the process for selecting presidential nominees is a major factor in determining who wins. This book presents a similar argument, even though the nomination process is dramatically different now than it was during Bryce's day. So we ask the question: What kind of person is likely to succeed in the current nomination process, and is such a person likely to be a successful president? Recent history suggests that three types of people have the potential to win a presidential nomination.

One is an established party leader. In chapters 6 and 7, we demonstrated that front-runners win, and that front-runners are usually identifiable as soon as they enter the race. In order to achieve instant front-runner status, a candidate has to be a well-respected figure in the party. He can earn that respect by having been chosen for a legislative leadership position. Alternatively, he may have established himself as the leader of a major ideological faction within the party. In either case, such a leader has proved his ability over an extended period of time, perhaps decades. He has been tested in battle and come out victorious.

The second type of person advantaged by the system is the sitting vice president. No sitting vice president who has sought his party's presidential nomination has been denied it since 1952, when the aging Alben Barkley, Truman's vice president, did not get the nod. The criteria for choosing a vice president are very different from those by which other party leaders are chosen. The vice president is handpicked by the presidential nominee shortly before the national convention. Each presidential candidate has his own criteria for choosing a running mate, but they generally include an assessment of which candidate will be most helpful in winning the election. Thus, vice presidents are chosen not by the collective judgment of the party but according to the particular needs of a presidential candidate.

The third and final type is the candidate who emerges from the pack to claim the mantle, either before or during the primary season. Such a candidate has to have developed a coherent message that inspires people to contribute time and money to the campaign. He has to have won over the party's major constituent groups and managed the media effectively. He also has to have demonstrated that he has both a strong political base and the ability to win support from others. In short, he has to be a first-rate politician.

The study of politics is sometimes compared to the making of sausage. Once you learn the details of how it works, you lose your appetite for the product. In this book, we have examined in great detail the process by which presidential nominees are selected. After looking at it up close, it is hard to believe that such a process could be expected to yield a highly qualified president.

Yet perhaps we should step back for a moment and examine the outcome. The presidential nominee is likely to be someone who has worked his way up through the party ranks until he has earned a leadership position. Or, he is a highly skilled politician. Or, he is a vice president who has had four to eight years of first-hand experience in the White House. On the whole, that is a pretty good set of qualifications for the president of the United States.

Index